© 2023 Jessica Bowman / AskMamaJ.com

All rights reserved. No part of this book may be reproduced in any form or by any electronic or mechanical means, including information storage and retrieval systems, without permission in writing from the publisher, except by a reviewer who may quote brief passages in a review.

Published by: Jessica Bowman

Cover design by: Jessica Bowman

Trenton, GA 30752

ISBN: 979-886-209810-5

Printed in the United States of America

For JJ and D, no matter where you are, I will never stop teaching and loving you!

In remembrance of my mother, Kay Wallin: 1963-2022

table of contents

Chapter 1: So...You're an Adult. Now What?!___5

Chapter 2: Getting Organized - Goal Setting Like a Pro___18

Chapter 3: Finding Your Dream Job 26

Chapter 4: Managing Your Money_ 44

Chapter 5: Cleaning like you mean it_ 66

Chapter 6: Cooking Basics___98

Chapter 7: Roommate Rules___120

Chapter 8: Self Care___147

Chapter 9: Summary___161

Chapter 10: Conclusion___170

Want more?___ 172

Acknowledgements___ 173

introduction

SO...YOU'RE AN ADULT.
NOW WHAT?!

Chapter 1: So...You're an Adult. Now What?!

"Don't abandon your dreams just because you grew up."

Mama J, AskMamaJ.com

Congratulations...you made it to adulthood.

But...what does that even mean?! And what do you do now?

Hi, I'm Mama J, and I'll be your guide throughout this book. Think of me like a wacky aunt or "bonus mom" who knows how hard it can be when you're just starting out in the "real world."

The world expects you to already know everything and has little patience or compassion for what you don't know. That thought alone can be pretty daunting.

With a little know-how and encouragement, you can enter the adult world confidently and be on your way to living your dreams. I'm here to help because I see you. The kid who maybe didn't have the best homelife growing up, or maybe your parents were always working, and they didn't have time to teach you these real world fundamentals.

And so here you are, at the precipice between childhood and adulthood. **And you're scared to death.**

I'm here to tell you that it doesn't have to be scary. I'm here to give you love and encouragement as you embark on this amazing journey. I'm here to give you the tools you need to succeed. I'm here, not to crush your childhood dreams, but to help you foster and nurture them into grown-up realities.

I'm here because I want you to have an amazing life, no matter what life has been like leading up to now.

What does it mean to be an adult?

There's no one answer to the question of what it means to be an adult. It's a complex concept that can mean different things to different people.

However, there are some common characteristics that are often associated with adulthood. These include:

Taking responsibility for your own life

Adults are responsible for their own decisions, actions, and well-being. They make their own choices and live with the consequences.

Being financially independent

Adults are able to support themselves financially. They have a job or other source of income, and they are able to pay their bills and other expenses.

Being able to manage your time and resources

Adults are able to manage their time effectively and make wise decisions about how to use their resources. They are able to set priorities and achieve their goals.

Being able to form and maintain relationships

Adults are able to form and maintain healthy relationships with friends, family, and significant others. They are able to communicate effectively and resolve conflict in a constructive way.

Being able to make informed decisions

Adults are able to gather information and weigh different options before making decisions. They are able to think critically and make decisions that are in their best interests.

Of course, not all adults will exhibit all of these characteristics. However, these are some of the common characteristics that are often associated with adulthood.

Ultimately, what it means to be an adult is up to each individual to decide.

Here are some things to keep in mind about your new grown up status:

- **Adulthood is a journey, not a destination.** It is a process of growth and development that continues throughout your life.

- **There is no one right way to be an adult.** What matters most is that you are happy and fulfilled with your life.
- **Adulthood is not always easy.** There will be challenges and setbacks along the way. But it's also a time of great opportunity and growth.
- **If you're struggling with adulthood, you're not alone.** Many people feel lost or confused at some point in their lives. There are resources available to help you, such as therapy or support groups.

The challenges of adulthood

Adulthood is a time of great change and challenge. Here are some of the challenges that adults often face:

Financial independence

Adults are responsible for their own financial well-being. This means having a job or other source of income, and being able to pay their bills and other expenses.

Career development

Adults need to develop their careers and find work that is fulfilling and rewarding. This can be challenging, as the job market is constantly changing and there's a lot of competition.

Relationships

Adults need to maintain healthy relationships with friends, family, and significant others. This can be a challenge, as people's lives change and priorities shift over time.

Personal growth

Adults need to continue to grow and develop as individuals. This means learning new things, taking on new challenges, and reflecting on their experiences.

Mental and physical health

Adults need to take care of their mental and physical health. This means eating healthy, exercising regularly, and getting enough sleep.

Decision-making

Adults need to make important decisions about their lives, such as where to live, what career to pursue, and whether or not to have children. These decisions can be difficult, as there is no right or wrong answer.

These are just some of the challenges that adults often face. It is important to remember that everyone's experience of adulthood is different.

Some people may find these challenges easier to manage than others. However, it is important to be aware of these challenges and to seek help if you are struggling.

How to deal with adult problems

- **Set realistic goals**: Don't try to do too much too soon. Set small, achievable goals for yourself and gradually work your way up to larger goals.
- **Take care of yourself**: Make sure you're getting enough sleep, eating healthy foods, and exercising regularly. Taking care of your physical and mental health will help you cope with stress and make better decisions.
- **Ask for help**: If you're struggling, don't be afraid to ask for help from friends,

family, or a professional. There are people who care about you and want to help you succeed.
- **Be patient**: Adulthood is a journey, not a destination. It takes time to learn and grow. Be patient with yourself and don't expect to have everything figured out overnight.

Remember, you're not alone. Many people face challenges in adulthood. The important thing is to stay positive and keep moving forward. With hard work and dedication, you can overcome any challenge.

How to embrace adulthood

Adulthood is a time of great change and opportunity. It can be a bit daunting at first, but it can also be a lot of fun. Here are some ways to embrace adulthood:

- **Take ownership for your life**: This means making your own decisions,

taking care of your responsibilities, and learning from your mistakes.
- **Set goals and work towards them**: Having goals will give you something to strive for and help you stay motivated.
- **Learn new things**: There are endless opportunities to learn new things, both inside and outside of school. Learning new things will help you grow as a person and make you more interesting.
- **Take care of your health**: This means eating healthy, exercising regularly, and getting enough sleep. Taking care of your health will help you feel your best and have more energy.
- **Build strong relationships**: Strong relationships with friends, family, and significant others will provide you with support and happiness.
- **Give back to your community**: There are many ways to give back to your community, such as volunteering your time or donating to charity. Giving back will make you feel good and make a difference in the world.

- **Have fun!** Adulthood is a time to enjoy life and experience new things. Don't be afraid to let loose and have fun.

Keep in mind:

- **Be patient:** It takes time to adjust to adulthood. Don't expect to have everything figured out overnight.
- **Be kind to yourself:** Adulthood can be challenging, but it's important to be kind to yourself and to forgive yourself for your mistakes.
- **Ask for help:** If you're struggling, don't be afraid to ask for help from friends, family, or a professional.
- **Enjoy the journey:** Adulthood is a journey, not a destination. Soak up every moment and enjoy the ride.

Remember: you're not going to get everything right, all the time. But making mistakes can be one of the best ways to learn and grow as an adult, and it's important to give yourself grace when things go awry.

Lessons and blessings

One way to thrive in adulthood is to look for the "lessons and blessings" in every **misstep.** What did you learn from your mistakes? What were the silver linings? What did you take away from this experience?

Looking for the lessons and blessings can make a huge difference in your self-esteem and confidence in making decisions moving forward.

Points to remember:

- Being an adult means taking responsibility for your actions, and accepting the consequences.
- There's no one right way to be an adult, and everyone's journey is different.
- A big key to success in adulthood is proper planning and goal setting.
- Adulting is a journey, not a destination. Growing up doesn't happen overnight.
- When things go wrong, look for the lessons and blessings in the situation to avoid repeating mistakes.

GETTING ORGANIZED

GOAL SETTING LIKE A PRO

Chapter 2: Getting Organized - Goal Setting Like a Pro

"An ounce of prevention is worth a pound of cure."

Benjamin Franklin

How to get organized

Getting organized can be a daunting task, but it is essential for maintaining a healthy and productive lifestyle. When you're organized, you can find what you need when you need it, which saves you time and stress. You can also be more productive, as you will not have to waste time searching for things.

In this chapter, we will discuss some tips on how to get organized. We will cover topics such as decluttering, creating a system for organizing your belongings, and setting up a filing system. We will also discuss some digital organizing tips, such as using cloud storage and creating to-do lists.

By following the tips in this chapter, you can get organized and start living a more productive and stress-free life.

Create a system that works for you

The first step to getting organized is to create a system that works for you. This means finding a system that you can stick to and that helps you stay on top of your tasks.

There are many different organizational systems out there, so it's important to experiment and find one that works for you. Some popular organizational systems include:

- The Getting Things Done (GTD) system

- The Bullet Journal system
- The Kanban system

Once you've chosen a system, take some time to set it up. This may involve creating lists, calendars, or other tools.

Set goals and track your progress

Another way to get organized is to set goals and track your progress. This will help you stay motivated and on track.

When you set goals, be sure to make them specific, measurable, achievable, relevant, and time-bound (SMART). This will help you stay focused and make sure that your goals are realistic.

Once you've set your goals, track your progress regularly. This will help you see how you're doing and make sure that you're on track to achieve your goals.

Here are some tips for tracking your progress:

- Use a journal or app to track your progress.
- Set regular check-in dates to review your progress.
- Celebrate your successes along the way.

Stay motivated

Finally, it's important to stay motivated when you're trying to get organized. This can be challenging, but there are a few things you can do to stay on track.

- **Set small, achievable goals.** This will help you feel a sense of accomplishment and keep you motivated.
- **Reward yourself for your successes.** This will help you stay motivated and on track.
- **Find a support system.** This could be a friend, family member, or online

community. Having people to support you can help you stay motivated and on track.

I hope these tips help you get organized in your own life. Remember, getting organized takes time and effort, but it's worth it in the long run.

Find your why

One of the best ways to stay motivated is to find your why. This is your reason for wanting to achieve your goals. When you know your why, it will be easier to stay on track when things get tough.

Break down your goals into smaller steps

Another way to stay motivated is to break down your goals into smaller steps. This will make your goals seem less daunting and more achievable.

When you break down your goals, be sure to make the steps specific, measurable, achievable, relevant, and time-bound (SMART). This will help you stay focused and make sure that your goals are realistic.

Celebrate your successes

Finally, it's important to celebrate your successes along the way. This will help you stay motivated and on track.

When you celebrate your successes, be sure to do something that you enjoy. This could be anything from going out for a coffee to taking a day off.

Here are some other tips for staying motivated:

- **Visualize your success.** Imagine yourself achieving your goals and how

it will feel. This will help you stay motivated when things get tough.
- **Set realistic goals.** If your goals are too difficult, you're more likely to give up. Set goals that you know you can achieve with hard work and dedication.
- **Take breaks.** Don't try to do too much at once. Take breaks throughout the day to recharge and stay motivated.
- **Find a support system.** Having people to support you can help you stay motivated and on track.

I hope these suggestions help you stay motivated in your own life. Remember, motivation is a journey, not a destination. There will be ups and downs along the way, but it's important to keep going.

Additional resources

- Free Monthly Goal Sheet - AskMamaJ.com
- [The Getting Things Done (GTD) system](#) -

askmamaj.com/go/getting-things-done
- [The Bullet Journal system](#)- askmamaj.com/go/bullet-journal-system
- [The Kanban system](#) - askmamaj.com/go/kanban
- [The Living Well Planner](#) - askmamaj.com/go/living-well-planner

---

Points to remember:

- Set goals and track your progress.
- It's important to find your "why," what motivates you to succeed
- Break big goals into smaller, more manageable ones
- Celebrate your wins!

finding your dream job

HOW TO GET ON THE PATH TOWARDS THE RIGHT CAREER

Chapter 3: Finding Your Dream Job

"Choose a job you love and you'll never have to work a day in your life"

Confucius

Where do you start?

Finding a job you love can be challenging, especially when you're first starting out in the workforce. You may not have a lot of experience or connections, and you may not know where to start.

But don't worry, I have a few tricks you can implement to increase your chances of finding a job you'll love. If you've ever searched for a job in the past, you might have done it the traditional way, where you searched for places in your area that were hiring and tried to find something that matched your skillset and your income requirements.

Well, spoiler alert: we're about to rock the boat!

Brainstorming time!

First, spend 5-10 minutes writing down what you would do if you won a billion dollars.

This exercise can help you identify your passions and values. What would you spend your money on? Who would you help? What would you do with your time?

The answers to these questions can give you some clues about what kind of work you would be passionate about.

Next, spend 10-15 minutes writing down all of the companies, brands, organizations, and people you admire most.

This exercise can help you identify companies and organizations that share your values. What companies do you find yourself shopping at over and over again? What companies do you think are doing great things for the world?

The answers to these questions can help you identify companies that you would be excited to work for.

Finally, brainstorm what you enjoy doing most, what you are best at, and where the items overlap.

This exercise can help you identify your strengths and interests. What are you good at? What do you enjoy doing?

The answers to these questions can help you narrow down your options and focus on jobs that are a good fit for you.

Time to research

Now that you've brainstormed, you can bypass looking for places that are hiring and stick to the list of potential places you already admire. Begin by searching their websites for employment opportunities.

If you're passionate about a particular company or brand, don't wait for them to post a job opening. Reach out to them directly and express your interest in working for them.

You can send a polite professional letter or email introducing yourself and telling them about your love and admiration for their company or brand. Include some strengths you have that might be valuable to them, and offer to send your resume in a second email if they are interested.

Even if there are no job openings at the moment, you never know when a position might come up. By reaching out to your dream companies, you can get your foot in the door and let them know that you're interested in working for them.

Get after it

Repeat until you have a job that you love! Don't be afraid to follow up more than once. And keep in mind, just because a company or brand can't use you right now, doesn't mean you won't stick out in their mind when they are looking for someone.

Finding a job you love takes time and effort, but it's definitely possible. Don't give up, and keep following your passions. With hard work and determination, you'll eventually find the perfect job for you.

Here are some additional tips for finding a job you love:

- **Network with people who are already working in your desired field.** This is a great way to learn more about the industry and to get your foot in the door.
- **Don't be afraid to take on unpaid internships or volunteer work.** This is a great way to gain experience and to make connections in your desired field.
- **Be persistent.** Don't give up if you don't find a job right away. Keep applying for jobs and networking, and eventually you'll find the perfect job for you.

Here is a sample letter template that you can send to your favorite companies, whether they are hiring or not!

Sample letter template:

Dear [Hiring Manager name],

I am writing to express my interest in working for [Company name]. I have been a long-time admirer of your company and its mission, and I believe that my skills and experience would be a valuable asset to your team.

I have been following [Company name] for many years, and I am consistently impressed by your commitment to [Company mission]. I am particularly interested in your work in [Specific area of interest]. I believe that my skills in [Your skills] would be a valuable addition to your team, and I am confident that I could make a significant contribution to your company's mission.

In addition to my skills, I am also a highly motivated and results-oriented individual. I am confident that I could quickly learn the ropes and make a positive impact on your team. I am also a team player and I am eager to learn from others.

I would be happy to provide you with my resume or additional information and answer any questions you may have. I am available to chat at your convenience. My phone number is XXX-XXX-XXXX, or you can simply reply to this email.

Thank you for your time and consideration. I look forward to hearing from you soon.

Sincerely,

YOUR NAME

Additional letter writing tips

Here are a few more ways to ensure you send a memorable and professional letter:

Be personal and specific.

Don't just send a generic letter that could be sent to any company. Take the time to research the company and personalize your letter to show that you're genuinely interested in working for them.

Be clear about your skills and experience.

Highlight the skills and experience that would make you a valuable asset to the company.

Be enthusiastic.

Show your enthusiasm for the company and its mission.

Be professional.

Proofread your letter carefully before sending it.

Finding a job you love can be a daunting task, especially when you're just starting out in your career. But it's important to remember that you're not alone. Many young adults feel the same way.

Finally, don't be afraid to reach out to companies you admire. If you're passionate about a particular company or brand, don't wait for them to post a job opening. Reach out to them directly and express your interest in working for them.

Finding your dream job takes time and effort, but it's definitely possible. Don't give up, and keep following your passions. With hard work and determination, you'll eventually find the perfect job for you.

More ways to snag your dream job

- **Be patient.** It may take some time to find the perfect job. Don't give up, and keep searching.
- **Don't be afraid to take risks.** Sometimes you have to take risks to find the perfect job. Don't be afraid to step outside of your comfort zone and try something new.
- **Believe in yourself.** You can do this! Believe in yourself and your ability to find the perfect job.

Nailing your job interview

Okay, you've found your dream job, and you've landed an interview! Now what??

Do your research

- **Learn about the company**: Before your interview, take some time to learn about the company. This includes their history, their products or services, and their culture. You can find this information on the company's website, social media pages, and news articles.
- **Research the position**: In addition to learning about the company, you should also research the position you are applying for. This includes the responsibilities of the position, the skills and experience required, and the company's expectations. You can find this information on the job posting, the company's website, and job boards.

Practice your answers to common interview questions

There are a few common interview questions that you can expect to be asked. These include questions about your experience, your skills, and why you are interested in the position. You can practice your answers to these questions by yourself or with a friend or family member.

Be prepared to answer questions about your weaknesses. When asked about your weaknesses, be honest but also be sure to focus on how you are working to improve them.

Be prepared to answer questions about your salary expectations. When asked about your salary expectations, do some research to find out what the average salary is for the position in your area. You can also ask your recruiter for guidance.

Dress professionally

First impressions matter, so make sure you dress professionally for your interview. This means wearing clean, pressed clothes that are appropriate for the company culture.

Avoid wearing anything too casual, too revealing, or too flashy. You want to look professional and put-together, but you don't want to overdress.

If you're not sure what to wear, err on the side of caution and dress more conservatively. You can always dress down after you get the job.

Here are some additional tips for acing your job interview:

- **Be on time**: Punctuality is important, so make sure you arrive for your interview on time.
- **Be polite and respectful**: Address the interviewer by their title and last name, and be sure to thank them for their time at the end of the interview.

- **Be confident:** Believe in yourself and your abilities. Show the interviewer that you are confident in your skills and that you are excited about the position.
- **Be yourself:** Don't try to be someone you're not. The interviewer wants to get to know the real you, so be yourself and let your personality shine through.

One of the most important ways to land the job of your dreams is to **focus on how you will add value to the company.** Instead of asking "what's in it for me," focus on "here's what I can do for you." When you make it to the second or third interview, then you can inquire about the various benefits the company has to offer.

I hope these tips help you ace your next job interview!

Starting your new job off on the right foot

Congratulations, you've landed your dream job! Or, at least, *A* job. Now what?! How do you keep it?

Be on time

- Punctuality is important in any job, but it's especially important when you're starting a new job. Arriving on time shows your employer that you're reliable and that you take your job seriously.
- If you're going to be late, be sure to call or email your employer as soon as possible. This will give them a heads up and allow them to adjust their plans accordingly.

Most businesses consider arriving 10 minutes early to be "on time" and arriving on time as "late." Some companies may be more lenient, but arriving just a few minutes early gives you time to get organized and settled and better prepared for your workday.

Be prepared

- Before your first day of work, take some time to familiarize yourself with the company and the position. This includes reading the company's website, learning about the company's products or services, and reviewing the job description.
- If you have any questions, be sure to ask your employer or your co-workers. They will be happy to help you get up to speed.

Be respectful

- Respect your employer, your co-workers, and the customers or clients you interact with. This means

being polite, being on time, and being professional.
- Be open to feedback and be willing to learn. Your employer and your co-workers will be more likely to help you if you're willing to listen to their advice.

Here are some additional tips for starting your new job off on the right foot:

Be positive and enthusiastic.

Show your employer that you're excited to be there and that you're eager to learn.

Be a team player.

Be willing to help out your co-workers and be supportive of the team's goals.

Be willing to go the extra mile.

If you're willing to put in the extra effort, your employer will notice and appreciate it.

Points to remember:

- Finding your dream career path is simplified with a little bit of brainstorming.
- Impress upon potential supervisors the value you would bring to your dream company or business.
- Be professional and positive.

managing your money

HOW TO MAKE A BUDGET, SAVE FOR THE FUTURE, & PAY OFF DEBT

Chapter 4: Managing Your Money

"Do not save what is left after spending, but spend what is left after saving."

Warren Buffet

How to make a budget, save for the future, and pay off debt

Managing your money is an essential skill for everyone. Whether you're just starting out or you are a seasoned pro, there are always ways to improve your financial situation.

In this chapter, we'll discuss some tips on how to manage your money effectively. We will cover topics such as making a budget, saving for the future, and paying off debt.

We will also discuss some of the challenges that people face when managing their money, such as impulse spending and living beyond their means. We will provide some tips on how to overcome these challenges and achieve your financial goals.

By following the tips in this chapter, you can learn how to manage your money effectively and reach your financial goals.

How to deal with money when you're just starting out

One of the most important things you'll need to learn as an adult is how to manage your money. This chapter will give you some tips on how to do just that.

We'll start by talking about how to deal with money when you're just starting out. Then, we'll discuss creating a budget, starting saving for the future, paying off debt, using credit cards wisely, and some tips not to do. Finally, we'll provide you with some additional resources to help you learn more about managing your money.

Here are a few ways to handle money when you're just starting out:

Open a bank account

This is the first step to managing your money. You'll need a bank account to deposit your paychecks and pay your bills.

Set up a budget

A budget is a plan for how you're going to spend your money. It can help you track your income and expenses, and make sure you're not spending more than you make.

Start saving for the future

Even if you can only save a little bit each month, it's a good idea to start saving for the future. This could mean saving for a down payment on a house, retirement, or your child's education.

Pay off debt

If you have debt, it's important to pay it off as quickly as possible. The longer you have debt, the more interest you'll pay.

Use credit cards wisely

Credit cards can be a great way to build your credit score, but they can also be a trap if you're not careful. Only use credit cards for things you can afford to pay off in full each month, and never carry a balance from month to month.

Opening a bank account

Here are some things to keep in mind when opening a bank account:

- **Do your research.** There are many different banks and credit unions out there, so it's important to do your research and find one that's right for you. Consider factors such as the interest rates they offer, the fees they charge, and the location of their branches.
- **Compare offers.** Once you've found a few banks that you're interested in, compare their offers. This includes the interest rates they offer on savings accounts, the fees they charge for checking accounts, and any other fees they may charge.
- **Consider your needs.** Think about your financial needs and what you'll be using the bank account for. If you're going to be using the account to deposit your paychecks and pay your bills, you'll need a checking

account. If you're saving for the future, you'll need a savings account.
- **Open the account online or in person.** Most banks allow you to open an account online. However, if you're not comfortable doing this, you can also open an account in person at a branch.
- **Bring the necessary documents.** When you open a bank account, you'll need to bring some basic documents with you. This may include your driver's license, Social Security card, and proof of address.
- **Set up direct deposit.** If you have a job, you can set up direct deposit so that your paychecks are deposited directly into your bank account. This will save you the hassle of having to deposit your checks yourself.
- **Set up bill pay.** You can also set up bill pay so that your bills are automatically paid from your bank account. This will help you avoid late fees and keep track of your bills.

Creating a budget

Creating a budget is the most important thing you can do to manage your money. A budget will help you track your income and expenses, so you can see where your money is going. There are many different budgeting apps and software programs available, so you can find one that works for you.

Creating a budget is the most essential thing you can do to manage your money because it gives you a clear picture of your financial situation. Once you know where your money is going, you can start to make changes to your spending habits and reach your financial goals.

There are many different ways to create a budget. You can use a budgeting app, software program, or even just a spreadsheet. The principal thing is to find a method that works for you and that you're willing to stick to.

Here are some tips for creating a budget:

- Start by tracking your income and expenses for one month. This will give you a good idea of where your money is going.
- Once you know your income and expenses, you can start to create categories for your spending. Some common categories include housing, transportation, food, entertainment, and debt payments.
- Set a budget for each category. This will help you stay on track and avoid overspending.
- Be realistic with your budget. Don't try to cut your spending too much in the beginning. Start with small changes and gradually make more adjustments as you get used to your budget.
- Review your budget regularly and make adjustments as needed. Your budget should be a living document that you can update as your financial situation changes.

Pay your bills first

Pay bills first. This is one of the most essential financial rules to follow. Your bills should be your top priority, as they are essential for your survival and well-being.

When it comes to paying bills, it's fundamental to prioritize them. The primary bills to pay first are your housing costs (rent or mortgage), utilities, and car payment. These are the bills that will keep a roof over your head, the lights on, and keep you mobile.

Once you've paid your essential bills, you can then focus on paying other bills, such as credit card debt, student loans, and other debts. You can also start to save money for the future.

Paying bills by priority

Don't have enough money for everything you want, and need to prioritize? Focus on your bills in this order, and you will be back on your feet in no time!

1. **Housing costs.** This includes your rent or mortgage payment, as well as any associated costs, such as property taxes or homeowners insurance.
2. **Utilities.** This includes your water, gas, electric, and trash removal bills.
3. **Car payment.** If you have a car, your car payment is another essential bill to pay.
4. **Groceries, gas, & toiletries.** You need to eat, and you need to be able to get around. And you definitely need toilet paper.
5. **Cell phone/internet bill.** There's not much we can do these days without our phone or computer!
6. **Debt payments.** If you have any debt, such as credit card debt or student loans, you should start paying it off as soon as possible.

7. **Savings**. Once you've paid your essential bills and started to pay down your debt, you can start to save money for the future.
8. **Activities, clothing, & everything else**. Try to have a certain number in mind when buying additional items. You don't have to live paycheck to paycheck, but it's very easy to do. By setting a standard amount for each month, you will quickly discover what you really need, and what you don't.

It's key to note that this is just a general order of priority. Your specific financial situation may warrant a different order of priority. For example, if you have a high-interest credit card debt, you may want to prioritize paying that debt off before you pay off your car loan.

The most essential thing is to make sure that you're paying your bills on time and in full. This will help you avoid late fees and damage your credit score.

start saving for the future

Even if you can only save a small amount of money each month, it will add up over time. Start by setting a goal for yourself, such as saving for a down payment on a house or retirement.

Starting to save for the future is one of the best things you can do for your financial well-being. Even if you can only save a small amount of money each month, it will add up over time. The earlier you start saving, the more time your money has to grow.

Here are some ways you can start saving for the future NOW:

- **Set a goal.** What are you saving for? A down payment on a house? Retirement? Once you know your goal, you can start to figure out how much you need to save each month.
- **Automate your savings.** The best way to make sure you're saving money each month is to automate your savings. This means setting up a

direct deposit from your paycheck into your savings account.
- **Choose a high-yield savings account.** Not all savings accounts are created equal. Some offer higher interest rates than others. Do some research to find a high-yield savings account that will help your money grow.
- **Be patient.** Saving for the future takes time and effort. Don't get discouraged if you don't see results overnight. Just keep at it, and you'll eventually reach your financial goals.

Paying off debt

If you have any debt, make it a priority to pay it off as quickly as possible. The longer you carry debt, the more interest you'll pay.

There are two main methods for paying off debt: **the snowball method and the avalanche method.**

The snowball method

The snowball method is a debt payoff method where you focus on paying off your smallest debts first, regardless of the interest rate. Once you pay off a debt, you roll the amount you were paying towards that debt into the payment for your next smallest debt. This process continues until all of your debts are paid off.

The snowball method can be a great way to stay motivated and make progress on your debt, as you'll see your debts disappear one by one. However, it's fundamental to note that the snowball method may not be the most efficient way to pay off debt, as you may end up paying more interest in the long run.

The avalanche method

The avalanche method is a debt payoff method where you focus on paying off your debts with the highest interest rates first.

This method may not be as motivating as the snowball method, but it is the most efficient way to pay off debt, as you'll save the most money in interest.

The best debt payoff method for you will depend on your individual circumstances and preferences. If you're motivated by seeing progress, the snowball method may be a good option for you. If you're more concerned with paying off debt as quickly as possible, the avalanche method may be a better choice.

Got debt? Here's how to make it go away:

- **Create a budget.** This will help you track your income and expenses, so you can see how much money you have available to pay off your debt.
- **Make a list of your debts.** Include the balance, interest rate, and minimum payment for each debt.
- **Prioritize your debts.** Decide which debt you want to pay off first. You can use the snowball method or the avalanche method.

- **Make a plan.** Decide how much money you can afford to pay towards your debt each month.
- **Stick to your plan.** It's key to be consistent with your payments.
- **Get help if you need it.** There are many resources available to help you pay off debt. You may want to consider talking to a financial advisor or joining a debt-free community.

Paying off debt can be a challenge, but it's definitely possible. By following these tips, you can reach your financial goals and become debt-free.

use credit cards wisely (or not at all)

Credit cards can be a great way to build your credit score, but only if you use them responsibly. Pay your bills on time and in full each month, and don't spend more than you can afford to pay back.

Here are some of the dangers of credit cards:

- **High interest rates**: Credit cards typically have high interest rates, which means you'll pay a lot of money in interest if you don't pay your bill in full each month.
- **Late fees**: If you don't pay your bill on time, you'll be charged a late fee. These fees can be expensive, and they can damage your credit score.
- **Overspending**: It's easy to overspend with a credit card, especially if you're not careful. If you don't track your spending, you could end up in debt.
- **Fraud**: Credit card fraud is a real problem, and it can be difficult to get your money back if your card is stolen.

Avoid these credit card pitfalls:

- Only use credit cards for purchases you can afford to pay back in full each month.
- Set up automatic payments so you never miss a bill payment.
- Track your spending so you don't overspend.
- Be aware of the risks of fraud and take steps to protect yourself.

If you use credit cards wisely, they can be a great way to build your credit score and make purchases. However, it's important to be aware of the dangers and take steps to protect yourself.

Here are some more tips for using credit cards wisely:

- Read the terms and conditions of your credit card carefully before you sign up. This will help you understand

the interest rates, fees, and other terms of your card.
- Choose a credit card that has a low interest rate and no annual fee. This will save you money in the long run.
- Use your credit card for everyday purchases, such as gas, groceries, and dining out. This will help you build your credit history.
- Pay your credit card bill on time and in full each month. This is the most important thing you can do to avoid interest charges and damage to your credit score.
- Don't carry a balance on your credit card. If you do, you'll pay interest on the balance, which can be expensive.
- Be aware of the risks of fraud. Keep your credit card number and PIN safe, and report any suspicious activity to your credit card company immediately.

By following these tips, you can use credit cards wisely and build a strong credit history.

Managing your money takes time and effort. Don't get discouraged if you don't see results overnight. Just keep at it, and you'll eventually reach your financial goals!

Avoid these money mishaps

- **Don't live beyond your means.** This is one of the biggest mistakes young adults make. If you spend more money than you earn, you'll quickly find yourself in debt.
- **Don't impulse buy.** It's easy to get caught up in the moment and buy things you don't need. Before you make a purchase, ask yourself if you really need it and if you can afford it.
- **Don't ignore your bills.** If you don't pay your bills on time, you'll damage your credit score and could even end up in collections.
- **Don't be afraid to ask for help.** If you're struggling to manage your money, don't be afraid to ask for help from a financial advisor or a trusted friend or family member.

- **Don't borrow more than you can repay.** Credit card interest rates are no joke! It's easy to get in over your head, and borrowing a little can turn into a lot with high interest rates and can take years to repay!

Managing your money is a lifelong journey. There will be ups and downs along the way, but by following these tips, you can set yourself up for financial success.

I hope this gives you a little bit of peace of mind! Of course there will be mistakes and mishaps, but it's much easier to start off on the right foot than it is to try to unlearn bad habits. You've got this!

Investing money wisely

Wanting to get a jump on investing, but not sure where to start? Here are some ways to invest your money wisely:

Do your research

- Before you invest any money, it's important to do your research. This means learning about different investment options, such as stocks, bonds, and mutual funds. You should also learn about the risks and rewards of each investment option.
- You can find information about investments on the internet, in books, and from financial advisors. It's important to get your information from reliable sources.

Start small

- If you're new to investing, it's a good idea to start small. This means investing a small amount of money that you can afford to lose.
- As you gain more experience, you can gradually increase the amount of money you invest. But it's important to start small so that you don't risk

losing too much money if the market takes a downturn.

Be patient

- Investing is a long-term game. This means that you shouldn't expect to get rich quickly.
- It takes time for investments to grow. So, it's important to be patient and not panic if the market takes a short-term downturn.

A few more things to remember when investing your money:

- **Diversify your portfolio.** This means investing in a variety of different investments. This will help to reduce your risk if one investment loses value.
- **Rebalance your portfolio regularly.** This means selling some of your winning investments and buying more of your losing investments. This will help to keep your portfolio balanced and reduce your risk.

- **Reinvest your dividends.** This means using the dividends you earn from your investments to buy more shares of the same investment. This will help your investments grow faster over time.

Managing your money wisely is an essential part of adulthood. If you are smart with your money, you can make a budget, save for the future, prioritize bills, pay off debt, and invest wisely. By doing these things, you will be on your way to financial freedom and success.

I hope this chapter has given you some helpful tips on how to manage your money wisely. Remember, financial freedom and success are within your reach if you are willing to put in the effort.

Additional Resources:

- The National Foundation for Credit Counseling -askmamaj.com/go/nfcc

- [The Consumer Financial Protection Bureau](askmamaj.com/go/consumer-finance)
  -askmamaj.com/go/consumer-finance
- [The Federal Trade Commission](askmamaj.com/go/ftc)
  -askmamaj.com/go/ftc

Points to remember:

- Don't live beyond your means—make sure to prioritize your necessities before you spend money on other things.
- Creating a budget will help you understand where your money is going and will put you on a path to financial success.
- Managing money is a lifelong journey. It may take decades to truly get into a good groove!

Cleaning Like You Mean It

HOW TO
CREATE A CLEANING ROUTINE,
TACKLE LARGE PROJECTS, &
KEEP YOUR HOME CLEAN

Chapter 5: Cleaning like you mean it

"When we clean and organize our space, we clean and organize our minds."

Mama J

How to create a cleaning routine, tackle large projects, and keep your home clean

Cleaning can be a daunting task, but it's essential for maintaining a healthy and comfortable home. When your home is clean, you can relax and enjoy your space without having to worry about dirt, dust, and clutter.

In this chapter, we'll discuss some tips on how to clean your home effectively. We'll cover topics such as creating a cleaning routine, tackling large projects, and keeping your home clean on a daily basis. We'll also discuss some of the challenges that people face when cleaning their homes, such as procrastination and lack of motivation. We'll also provide some ways to overcome these challenges and keep your home clean and organized.

By following the tips in this chapter, you can learn how to clean your home effectively and stay on top of the cleaning chores.

Creating a cleaning routine

Creating a cleaning routine can be a great way to keep your home clean and organized. It can also help you save time and energy, and it can be a great way to de-stress.

Start small

When you're first starting out, it's best to start small. Don't try to clean your entire house in one day. Start with one room or one task, and then gradually add more as you get more comfortable.

Set realistic goals

It's also important to set realistic goals for yourself. If you set your goals too high, you're more likely to get discouraged and give up. Start with small, achievable goals, and then gradually increase them as you get more comfortable.

Make it fun

Finally, it's important to make your cleaning routine fun. If you're not enjoying yourself, you're less likely to stick with it. Find ways to make your cleaning routine more enjoyable, such as listening to music or watching a TV show while you clean.

Ways to create a cleaning routine

- **Choose a time of day that works for you.** Some people prefer to clean in the morning, while others prefer to clean in the evening. Choose a time that you're most likely to stick to.
- **Find a system that works for you.** Some people like to clean by room, while others like to clean by task. Find a system that you're comfortable with and that works for your lifestyle.
- **Set a timer.** This will help you stay on track and make sure that you're not spending too much time cleaning.
- **Reward yourself.** When you complete a cleaning task, reward yourself with something you enjoy. This will help you stay motivated and on track.

Some fun cleaning games to try:

- **Laundry basketball**: This is a great way to have a little more fun while cleaning. Set up a laundry basket in the corner of the room and see how many dirty clothes you can throw into the basket from across the room. You can even assign points and turn it into a competition!
- **3 minutes to clean**: This is a great way to break down a large cleaning project into smaller, more manageable tasks. Play a song and see how many microtasks you can complete during that time. For example, you could load and unload the dishwasher, wipe down the counters, or pick up items off the floor.
- **Panning for gold**: This is a fun way to make cleaning the litter box a little more exciting. Pretend you're a gold miner and see how many clumps of litter you can find. The bigger the clump, the more valuable your "gold" is.
- **Cleaning bingo**: This is a fun way to make cleaning more fun and

interactive. Create a bingo board with different cleaning tasks on it. As you complete each task, mark it off your bingo board. The first person to get five in a row wins.
- **Cleaning scavenger hunt**: This is another way to have fun while cleaning. Hide different cleaning supplies around the house and have the kids find them. The first person to find all of the supplies wins.
- **Cleaning challenges**: There are many different cleaning challenges that you can find online. These challenges can help you to stay motivated and on track with your cleaning routine.

Don't forget: cleaning is always a little bit more fun if you are singing and/or dancing!

I hope these tips help you create a cleaning routine that works for you. Remember, cleaning doesn't have to be boring or tedious. With a little planning and effort, you can create a cleaning routine that is both effective and fun!

How to tackle big cleaning projects

Tackling big cleaning projects can be daunting, but it doesn't have to be. By breaking the project down into smaller tasks, setting a timer, and taking breaks, you can make the project seem less overwhelming and more achievable.

Break them down into smaller tasks

The first step to tackling a big cleaning project is to break it down into smaller tasks. This will make the project seem less daunting and more manageable.

For example, if you're cleaning your entire house, you could break the project down into rooms. Then, you could break each room down into smaller tasks, such as dusting, vacuuming, and mopping.

Set a timer

Once you've broken the project down into smaller tasks, set a timer for a specific amount of time. This will help you stay focused and on track.

For example, you could set a timer for 30 minutes and focus on dusting and vacuuming one room. Then, you could set the timer for another 30 minutes and focus on mopping the same room.

Take breaks

It's important to take breaks when you're cleaning. This will help you stay focused and avoid getting overwhelmed.

For example, you could take a 5-minute break every 20 minutes. During your break, you could get up and move around, stretch, or grab a drink of water.

Keep in mind when tackling big cleaning projects:

- **Start small.** Don't try to tackle the entire project at once. Start with a small area or task and then gradually work your way up.
- **Be realistic.** Set realistic goals for yourself. If you set your goals too high, you're more likely to get discouraged and give up.
- **Reward yourself.** When you complete a task, reward yourself with something you enjoy. This will help you stay motivated and on track.

When you incorporate a little bit of planning and time to celebrate into your cleaning routine, you can not only get more done, but you'll also have more fun!

Keeping your home clean

Keeping your home clean doesn't have to be a daunting task. By following a few simple tips, you can keep your home looking its best without spending hours each week cleaning.

Do a little bit each day

One of the best ways to keep your home clean is to do a little bit each day. This will help you avoid having to do a big cleaning project all at once.

For example, you could set aside 15 minutes each day to do some light cleaning. This could include things like dusting, vacuuming, or putting things away.

Put things away as you use them

Another way to keep your home clean is to put things away as you use them. This will help you avoid having clutter build up, which can make your home look messy and unkempt.

For example, if you use a dish, put it away in the dishwasher or sink as soon as you're done with it. This will help you avoid having dirty dishes pile up in the sink.

Don't let clutter build up

One of the biggest causes of a dirty home is clutter. Clutter can make your home look messy and unkempt, and it can also be a breeding ground for dust and dirt.

To avoid clutter, try to declutter your home on a regular basis. This could mean getting rid of old clothes, furniture, or other items that you no longer use.

Here are some other ways to keep your home clean:

- **Vacuum and mop regularly.** This will help to remove dirt, dust, and allergens from your home.
- **Dust furniture and surfaces.** This will help to keep your home looking its best.

- Take out the trash regularly. This will help to prevent odors and pests.
- Clean the kitchen and bathroom regularly. This is important to prevent the spread of bacteria.

By following these tips, you'll be able to keep your home clean. Remember, a little bit of effort each day can go a long way in keeping your home looking its best.

Laundry 101

There are many ways to do laundry, and over time you will find the systems that work for you. But in the meantime, I will try to make it as simple as possible!

First, let's start with some basics, like how to use a washer and dryer:

Operating a washer and dryer

Washing Machine:

- **Basic settings:** Most washers have a few basic settings, such as regular, delicate, and heavy duty. You can also choose the water temperature, the amount of detergent (½-¾ capful per load if using liquid, one scoop if using powder, and one pod if using pods), and whether or not to use fabric softener.
- **Sorting your clothes:** This may be a bit controversial, but **it's really not necessary to sort your clothes before washing them**. In the two decades that I have been throwing everything in the washing machine together, I have had ONE white shirt turn pink from a red washrag that were washed together. It turns out I actually liked the pink, so I just washed it with the washrag together again. As Bob Ross would say, there are no mistakes, just happy accidents!
- **Loading the washer:** When loading the washer, be sure not to cram it too full. It will be quicker and easier

to wash and dry two smaller loads than it will be one large mega load.
- **Running the washer:** Once the washer is loaded, you can start it by selecting the desired settings and pressing the start button.
- **Checking the washer:** Once the washer is finished, be sure to check the clothes to make sure they're clean. If they're not, you can run them through the washer again. Don't leave your clothing in the washing machine for more than an hour or two, or they will sour, and then you'll have to wash them again!

Dryer:

- **Basic settings:** Most dryers have a few basic settings, such as regular, delicate, and high heat. You can also choose the amount of time to dry the clothes. Most clothing gets dried in about 40-60 minutes.
- **Loading the dryer:** When loading the dryer, be sure to spread the clothes

out evenly. This will help the clothes to dry more evenly and prevent them from getting wrinkled. Again, don't overfill! Or you'll be running that dryer all damn DAY.
- **Running the dryer:** Once the dryer is loaded, you can start it by selecting the desired settings and pressing the start button.
- **Checking the dryer:** Once the dryer is finished, be sure to check the clothes to make sure they're dry. If they're not, you can run them through the dryer again.

Reading clothing tag symbols

The symbols on clothing tags are called care symbols, and they tell you how to wash, dry, and iron your clothes. They are a universal language that is used all over the world, so you can be sure that the symbols on your clothes will be understood by anyone who does your laundry.

Here are some of the most common care symbols:

- **Washing:** The washing symbol is a bathtub with a number inside it. The number tells you the maximum water temperature that you should use to wash the garment. For example, a number 40 inside the bathtub means that you should wash the garment in water that is no warmer than 40 degrees Celsius (104 degrees Fahrenheit).
- **Drying:** The drying symbol is a square with a circle inside it. The number inside the circle tells you the maximum heat setting that you should use to dry the garment. For example, a number 1 inside the circle means that you should tumble dry the garment on a low heat setting.
- **Ironing:** The ironing symbol is an iron with dots inside it. The number of dots tells you the maximum heat setting that you should use to iron

the garment. For example, a one-dot ironing symbol means that you can iron the garment on a low heat setting.

There are also a few other care symbols that you may see on clothing tags, such as symbols for bleaching, dry cleaning, and hand washing. These symbols are all pretty self-explanatory, but if you're ever unsure about what a symbol means, you can always consult a care label guide.

Pay attention to these things when reading care symbols:

- **The fabric type:** The fabric type of your garment will determine the care symbols that you need to follow. For example, wool garments should be washed and dried differently than cotton garments.
- **The care instructions:** The care instructions on the tag will tell you

exactly how to wash, dry, and iron your garment. Be sure to follow these instructions carefully to avoid damaging your clothes.
- **The condition of the garment:** If your garment is old or delicate, you may want to be more careful when washing and drying it. For example, you may want to wash it in cold water or hang it to dry instead of putting it in the dryer.

By paying attention to the care symbols on your clothing tags, you can help to keep your clothes looking their best for longer.

The point of folding clothes

Folding clothes helps to keep them wrinkle-free and organized. It also makes it easier to find the clothes you want to wear. If you're feeling lazy, you can always just toss your clothes in a drawer or basket, but they'll be more wrinkled and harder to find.

I recommend investing in a few clothing drawer divider organizers. They're not expensive, but they are a lifesaver! They make it SO easy to see at a glance what you have. I wish they had had them years ago!

What's the difference between a dryer sheet and fabric softener?

A dryer sheet is a scented sheet that is placed in the dryer with your clothes. It helps to reduce static cling and make your clothes smell nice.

Fabric softener is a liquid that is added to the wash water. It helps to soften your clothes and make them feel more luxurious. You can use them both, or neither! Modern detergents are so strong that your clothes will get clean and smell nice without them.

If you're worried about static cling, though, purchasing some dryer sheets or wool dryer balls might be helpful! What are dryer balls, you ask? They are balls that are about the size of tennis balls and are made of wool.

When you put one or two in your dryer with your wet clothes, they will bounce around, "beating" your clothes and making them softer and static-free. You can add a drop or two of essential oils onto the balls to help your clothes smell even nicer. I recommend a drop each of lavender and lemon. Dryer balls are also a great option because they are green, reusable, and much less expensive in the long run!

How do I know if my clothes are dry?

Once the dryer has finished, open the door and feel them to see if they're still damp. If your clothes are still damp, put them back in the dryer for a few more minutes. Again, adding a dry towel to the wet clothes will help them dry faster!

How do I take care of delicates?

Delicates are clothes that are made of soft fabrics, such as silk, wool, or lace. They should be washed on a gentle cycle and dried on a low heat setting. You can also use a mesh laundry bag to protect your delicates from getting caught on other clothes in the wash. If you are like me and don't have time/don't want to make time for caring for delicates, you can always skip buying clothing that needs special care!

How do I prevent my clothes from shrinking?

To prevent your clothes from shrinking, wash them in cold water and hang them to dry. You can also use a fabric softener, which will help to keep your clothes from shrinking and fading. Most clothing is pre-shrunk these days, but if you get a handmade sweater or something like that, you may want to ask if it needs to be washed in cold water or if it's dryer-safe.

How do I get rid of wrinkles?

There are a few ways to get rid of wrinkles. You can iron your clothes, but this can be time-consuming. **You can also hang your clothes in the bathroom while you take a hot shower.** The steam will help to remove the wrinkles. Or, you can put a dry towel in the dryer with your clothes. The towel will help to absorb the moisture and remove the wrinkles.

There are sprays out there that claim to release wrinkles, but I've never had much luck with those. The shower method is probably the best and the easiest! Or you could avoid clothing that is prone to wrinkles, like cotton, wool, and linen. If I ever buy a blouse that, after washing, needs to be ironed, I usually just end up donating it and opting for a wrinkle-free option instead. Ain't nobody got time for that!

How do I fold clothes?

There are many methods and styles when it comes to folding clothes. In the end, you'll probably develop a system and routine that works for you and your personal space.

I use a mix of styles that I've learned over the years, from what I learned during my high school JROTC days, to the training videos I watched working at Walmart teaching how they fold towels and clothing in their stores, to the KonMari method, which I have only discovered in the last few years.

Since the KonMari method is probably the easiest to teach and one of the most effective, I will share this method in this book.

The KonMari method is a popular way to fold clothes that is said to help you declutter and organize your closet. Here are some steps on how to fold clothes using the KonMari method:

Folding clothes using the KonMari method

- Start by sorting your clean clothes by type. This will make it easier to fold them.
- Fold each item of clothing in half lengthwise.
- Fold the sleeves in half and tuck them into the body of the shirt.
- Fold the shirt in thirds, lengthwise.
- Stand the shirt upright in your drawer.

Here are some specific steps on how to fold specific types of clothing using the KonMari method:

- **Shirts:** Fold shirts as described above.
- **Pants:** Fold pants in half lengthwise, then fold them into thirds lengthwise.
- **Underwear:** Fold underwear in thirds and then fold over.
- **Socks:** Place socks on top of each other. Fold socks in half and then in half again.

- **Towels:** Fold towels in half lengthwise, then fold them in half again lengthwise.
- **Bras:** Fold bras in half.
- **Undershirts:** Fold undershirts in half and then in half again.

If you want to learn more about the Konmari method, check out *Tidying Up* on Netflix or check out the book *The Life-Changing Magic of Tidying Up* by Marie Kondo.

Here are a few more tips to help make your laundry journey as simple as possible:

- Use clothes storage dividers to help you fold and put away your laundry.
- Don't separate darks and lights anymore. Modern detergents and machines can handle both colors together.
- Buy clothes that won't wrinkle so you can avoid ironing.

- Put a dry towel in the dryer to help your clothes dry faster.

I know you can do this! Just remember to take it one step at a time. And if you ever get overwhelmed, just ask me for help.

Washing Dishes 101

Realtalk: I'm pretty sure no one actually enjoys washing dishes. Even with games, it can feel pretty tedious and leave your hands all dry and pruny. Here are the basics so you can get it done quickly and get back to your awesome adult life.

Washing Dishes by Hand

1. Scrape any leftover food into the trash or compost.
2. Fill a sink or dishpan with hot water and a few drops of dish soap.

3. Wash dishes one at a time, starting with the cleanest and working your way to the dirtiest.
4. Use a soft sponge or dishcloth to scrub dishes, being careful not to scratch them.
5. Rinse dishes thoroughly under hot water to remove all soap residue.
6. Dry dishes with a clean towel or air dry them.

Using a Dishwasher

1. Scrape any leftover food into the trash or compost.
2. Load the dishwasher with dirty dishes, making sure to put the heaviest items on the bottom (plates, pots and pans) and the lightest items (cups, plastic items) on the top.
3. Add dishwashing detergent or detergent pod to the dispenser.
4. Close the dishwasher door and turn it on.
5. Once the dishwasher cycle is complete, unload the dishes and dry them.

Tips for using a Dishwasher

- To save water, only run the dishwasher when it's full. However, modern dishwashers are usually energy efficient, so running a half-full dishwasher uses less water than washing them by hand.
- If you have a dishwasher with a pre-wash cycle, you can use it to remove any stuck-on food.
- If you have hard water, you may need to use a water softener or rinse aid to prevent water spots on your dishes.
- It's important to clean your dishwasher every so often. To do this, run the dishwasher while it's empty and pour a little vinegar into the detergent dispenser. A drop or two of lemon essential oil will help out with the vinegary smell. Once the dishwasher has run the vinegar cycle, wipe it out with a wet cloth.

Cleaning a Cast Iron Skillet

This is the fastest and easiest way you can clean out a cast iron skillet:

- DO NOT try to wash a cast iron skillet in a dishwasher, or with dish soap!
- Make sure you have wiped out any grease or as many food particles as you can with a paper towel or dry cloth first.
- Place the cast iron skillet on a stove eye and turn on the heat.
- Sprinkle a generous amount of salt or baking soda into the pan and cover with a thin layer of water.
- When the water comes to a boil, use a dish scrubbing brush to work the salt around into the pan.
- Let the water cool down, then drain.
- Rinse the skillet thoroughly and wipe around the inside of the skillet with a paper towel or dish rag.
- Dry it immediately.
- You can also do this by using a washrag dipped in hot water instead of placing the skillet on the stove. The

hotter the water, the faster it breaks down any food particles (e.g. no scrubbing!).
- Cleaning with salt also helps to season the skillet. Once dry, dip a dishrag or paper towel in olive oil or other edible oil, and rub the inside and outside of the skillet until shiny. This will help to keep your skillet seasoned and prevent rust.

Cleaning a Coffee Pot

- To clean a coffee pot with ice and salt, fill the coffee pot with ice cubes and a generous pour of table salt.
- Shake the coffee pot around in a circular motion, letting the ice move the salt around the pot. Do this for a few minutes (it's fun!).
- Rinse the coffee pot thoroughly with hot water and use a dish rag or paper towel to wipe out the inside of the coffee pot. Dry it immediately.

Cleaning out a microwave

- Fill a cup or bowl with water, and a tablespoon of vinegar. If you have essential oils, consider adding a drop or two of lemon or lime essential oil to help make it smell nice.
- Place the bowl in the microwave and set the microwave timer to 10 minutes.
- After 10 minutes, grab a dishcloth or paper towel and dip it into the hot water. Wipe out the walls and the inside of the door. The steam from the water should make this very easy!
- If the turntable is still dirty, remove it and put it in the dishwasher.

Other cleaning basics:

Here are a few other basics that will turn you into a cleaning wizard in no time!

Dusting

1. Start at the top of the room and work your way down.
2. Dust surfaces with a dry cloth or feather duster.
3. Pay attention to all surfaces, including furniture, appliances, light fixtures, and ceiling fans.
4. If you have any dust-sensitive items, such as antiques or electronics, you may want to use a microfiber cloth or a vacuum with a soft brush attachment.

Vacuuming

1. Vacuum all hard floors, starting at the edges and working your way in.
2. Be sure to vacuum under furniture and appliances.
3. If you have carpet, vacuum it regularly to remove dirt, dust, and allergens.
4. Use a vacuum with a HEPA filter to trap small particles.

Mopping

1. Sweep or vacuum the floor to remove any large debris.
2. Fill a bucket with warm water and a few drops of floor cleaner.
3. Wring out a mop head or sponge until it is damp, not wet.
4. Mop the floor in long, overlapping strokes.
5. Rinse the mop head or sponge frequently in the bucket.
6. Blot dry the floor with a clean towel.

If you're trying to save time and effort, consider investing in a mop-vacuum, such as the Shark VacMop. It cuts mopping time in half, and reusable pads make it environmentally friendly, too!

Here are some additional tips for dusting, vacuuming, and mopping:

- Dust regularly to prevent dust from accumulating.
- Vacuum at least once a week.

- Mop as needed, or more often if you have pets or children.
- Use the right tools for the job.
- Be sure to clean your vacuum cleaner filters regularly.
- Store your cleaning supplies in a safe place.

Points to remember:

- Cleaning is a lot easier if you tidy up as you go.
- Cleaning can be less of a chore if you make a game out of it or find another way to make it fun.
- Discovering different cleaning hacks can make cleaning more effective and less time-consuming.

Cooking Basics

HOW TO COOK LIKE YOU KNOW WHAT YOU'RE DOING

Chapter 6: Cooking Basics

"The most indispensable ingredient of all good home cooking: love for those you are cooking for."

Sophia Loren

How to cook like you know what you're doing

Cooking is a basic life skill that everyone should know. It's not only a way to feed yourself, but it can also be a creative outlet and a way to connect with others. But where do you start? If you're new to cooking, or if you're just looking to brush up on your skills, then this chapter is for you.

In this chapter, we'll cover the basics of cooking, from how to cook a basic meal, to how to cook for a crowd. We'll also explain some of the more "weird" cooking terms that you might come across. By the end of this chapter, you'll have the knowledge you need to start cooking like a pro.

How to cook a basic meal

Cooking a basic meal can be a daunting task, especially if you're new to the kitchen. But with a little planning and preparation, it's actually quite easy. Here are some basic steps to follow:

1. **Choose a recipe.** There are many different recipes available online and in cookbooks. Choose one that is simple and easy to follow.
2. **Gather your ingredients.** Make sure you have all of the ingredients you need before you start cooking.
3. **Follow the instructions.** Read the recipe carefully and follow the instructions step-by-step.

4. **Be patient.** Cooking takes time, so be patient and don't rush.
5. **Enjoy your meal!** Once your meal is cooked, sit down and enjoy your hard work.

Choosing a recipe

When choosing a recipe, there are a few things to keep in mind:

- **The difficulty level of the recipe.** If you're a beginner, choose a recipe that is simple and easy to follow.
- **The ingredients you have on hand.** If you don't have all of the ingredients for a recipe, you may need to substitute some.
- **The time you have to cook.** Some recipes take longer to cook than others. Choose a recipe that fits your schedule.

Gather your ingredients

Once you've chosen a recipe, it's time to gather your ingredients. Make sure you have everything you need before you start cooking. If you're missing an ingredient, you may need to make a substitution.

Follow the instructions

The most important step in cooking a basic meal is to follow the instructions. Read the recipe carefully and follow each step step-by-step. If you're not sure what to do, ask for help from a more experienced cook.

Be patient

Cooking takes time, so be patient and don't rush. If you're feeling stressed, take a break and come back to the recipe later.

Enjoy!

Once your meal is cooked, sit down and enjoy your hard work. Be proud of yourself for cooking a basic meal!

Here are some additional tips for cooking a basic meal:

- **Start with simple recipes.** If you're new to cooking, start with simple recipes that have few ingredients. This will help you get the hang of cooking without getting overwhelmed.
- **Read the recipe carefully.** Before you start cooking, read the recipe carefully and make sure you understand all of the steps. This will help you avoid making mistakes.
- **Measure your ingredients carefully.** When measuring ingredients, be sure to use the correct measuring cups and spoons. This will ensure that your dish turns out the way it's supposed to.
- **Don't be afraid to experiment.** If you're not sure how to cook something,

experiment with different ingredients and cooking methods. You may be surprised at what you can create.
- **Have fun!** Cooking should be enjoyable. So relax, have fun, and experiment until you find recipes that you love.

An additional note about experimenting with recipes: a good rule of thumb is to follow a recipe exactly as it is written the first time around. That way you know the basics and what it's intended to taste like.

Try the recipe their way and make notes about what you liked or didn't like about the recipe. Did it need more or less of something? Did you feel it would have been better to swap out one component for another? Did the temperatures and times work for your stove or oven? Do you want to try subbing unhealthy ingredients with unhealthier ones? Follow your gut and try out your ideas. It may turn out better than ever!

Once you have the basics of a recipe down, then it will be easier to tailor to your specific needs and tastes.

Weird cooking terms: what do they mean??

Trying to read a recipe, and you have no idea how much is in a "pinch" or what you actually do when the recipe says to "fold in?" Here are some weird cooking terms, explained!

- **Against the grain**: to cut meat, fish, or poultry against the direction of the muscle fibers. This makes the meat more tender and easier to chew.
- **Baste**: To brush food with melted butter or oil while it is cooking. This helps to keep the food moist and flavorful.
- **Blanche**: To cook food briefly in boiling water, then immediately plunge it into cold water to stop the cooking process. This is often done to vegetables to preserve their color and texture.

- **Braise**: To cook meat in a covered pot with a small amount of liquid over low heat. This is a slow cooking method that results in tender, flavorful meat.
- **Confit**: To cook food in its own fat. This is a traditional French cooking method that results in very tender, flavorful meat.
- **Dash**: A very small amount of an ingredient, even smaller than a pinch.
- **Dice**: To chop an ingredient into small, uniform cubes.
- **Emulsify**: To combine two liquids that don't normally mix, such as oil and water. This is often done by whisking or beating the liquids together while adding a small amount of an emulsifier, such as mustard or egg yolk.
- **Filet**: To remove the bones and skin from a fish.
- **Fold in**: To combine two ingredients without deflating or overmixing them. This is often done when adding beaten egg whites or whipped cream to a batter or dough.
- **Glaze**: To coat food with a sweet or savory sauce before serving. This

helps to add flavor and moisture to the food.
- **Julienne**: To chop an ingredient into thin, matchstick-sized strips.
- **Jus**: The flavorful liquid that is left over after meat has been cooked. It can be used to make a sauce or to add flavor to other dishes.
- **Melt-in-your-mouth**: This term refers to food that is so tender that it literally melts in your mouth.
- **Mince**: To chop an ingredient into very small pieces.
- **Pan-fry**: To cook food in a pan over medium heat with a small amount of oil or butter. This is a quick and easy way to cook meat, poultry, or vegetables.
- **Panko**: A type of Japanese bread crumb that is used for frying. It is made from bread that has been dried and then crushed into small, coarse crumbs.
- **Poach**: To cook food in a simmering liquid. This is often done with delicate foods such as fish or eggs.
- **Reduce**: To cook a liquid over low heat until it has thickened. This is often

done to sauces or soups to concentrate the flavor.
- **Sauté**: To cook food in a pan over medium heat with a small amount of oil or butter. This is a quick and easy way to cook meat, poultry, or vegetables.
- **Simmer**: To cook food in a liquid that is just below the boiling point. This is often done to cook sauces or stews.
- **Sous vide**: A cooking technique that involves vacuum-sealing food and then cooking it in a water bath at a precise temperature.
- **Temper**: To slowly whisk eggs into a hot liquid to prevent them from curdling.
- **Tenderize**: To break down the tough muscle fibers in meat. This can be done by marinating, pounding, or brining the meat.

How to grocery shop

Grocery shopping can be a daunting task, especially if you're on a budget or trying to eat healthy. But with a little planning and preparation, you can make the process easier and more efficient.

Make a list

The first step to successful grocery shopping is to make a list of the items you need. This will help you stay focused and avoid impulse purchases. When making your list, be sure to include everything you need for the week, including staples like bread, milk, and eggs.

Stick to your list

Once you have your list, it's important to stick to it. This can be difficult, especially when you're faced with all the delicious temptations in the grocery store. But if you can resist the urge to stray from your list, you'll save money and avoid overeating.

Don't be afraid to ask for help

If you're not sure where to find an item or how to cook a certain dish, don't be afraid to ask for help from a store employee. They're there to help you, and they can often give you great tips on how to save money or find the best deals.

Here are some additional ways to save money and avoid common grocery store traps:

- **Shop at the right time.** Grocery stores often have sales and discounts at certain times of the day or week. If you can, try to shop during these times to save money.
- **Look for coupons and discounts.** There are many ways to find coupons and discounts for groceries. You can check the Sunday newspaper, online coupon websites, or even your local grocery store's website.
- **Buy in bulk.** If you have the space, buying in bulk can save you a lot of

money. Just be sure to use the items before they go bad.
- **Avoid impulse purchases.** It's easy to get caught up in the excitement of grocery shopping and end up buying things you don't need. To avoid this, only shop when you're not hungry and avoid browsing the aisles.

Next time you're grocery shopping, be sure to plan ahead, stick to your list, and don't be afraid to ask for help, and you'll be grocery shopping like a pro!

Making healthy choices when grocery shopping:

Looking to avoid falling into unhealthy marketing traps? Here are some ways to make healthier choices at the grocery store:

- **Shop the perimeter of the store.** The perimeter of the grocery store is where you'll find fresh produce, meat, dairy, and other healthy foods. These

foods are typically more expensive than processed foods, but they're also more nutritious.
- **Avoid the aisles.** The aisles of the grocery store are where you'll find processed foods, snacks, and sugary drinks. These foods are often cheaper than healthy foods, but they're also less nutritious.
- **Be aware of eye-level placement.** Many grocery stores place unhealthy foods at eye level, such as chips, cookies, and candy. This is because they know that people are more likely to buy these items if they're easy to see. To avoid these traps, shop from the bottom shelves or the top shelves.
- **Read labels carefully.** When you're buying processed foods, be sure to read the labels carefully. Look for foods that are low in sugar, salt, and unhealthy fats. Also, be sure to check the serving size. Many processed foods are high in calories, even when the serving size is small.
- **Avoid marketing gimmicks.** Grocery stores often use marketing tactics to get you to buy unhealthy foods disguised as healthy foods. They may

use the color green to make you feel like you're getting a healthy item. They may also use buzzwords like "gluten free," "low fat," or "keto" to get you to buy their product. Pay attention to the small print; it usually tells the real story that the larger print does not.

Here are some more ways to read labels and avoid marketing traps:

- **Look for the Nutrition Facts Panel.** The Nutrition Facts Panel is a standardized way of displaying the nutritional information for a food product. It includes information about calories, fat, sodium, carbohydrates, protein, and other nutrients.
- **Pay attention to serving size.** The serving size is the amount of food that the manufacturer considers to be one serving. Many processed foods are high in calories, even when the serving size is small.
- **Look for words like "light," "reduced fat," and "fat-free."** These words often mean that the food has had some of

the fat removed. However, these foods may still be high in calories or sugar.
- **Avoid foods with added sugar.** Added sugar is any sugar that is not naturally found in the food. It's often added to processed foods to make them taste sweeter.
- **Be aware of marketing terms like "healthy" and "natural."** These terms are not regulated, so they can mean different things to different people. It's important to read the label carefully to see what the food actually contains.

By being mindful of these marketing traps, you can be sure to make healthy choices when you're grocery shopping.

How to cook for one

Cooking for one can be a challenge, but it doesn't have to be. With a little planning and creativity, you can easily cook delicious and satisfying meals for yourself.

In this section, we'll discuss some tips on how to cook for one. We'll cover topics such as choosing recipes that are appropriate for one person, cooking in batches, and storing leftovers. We'll also provide some tips on how to make cooking for one more enjoyable.

Start with a plan.

Before you start cooking, take some time to plan your meal. This will help you to avoid wasting food and to make sure that you have everything you need.

Use leftovers.

If you're cooking for one, there's a good chance that you'll have leftovers. Leftovers are a great way to save time and money. You can eat them for lunch the next day or use them to make a new dish.

Cook in batches.

If you're cooking a dish that can be frozen, cook it in a large batch and freeze the leftovers. This way, you'll always have a quick and easy meal on hand.

Use small appliances.

Small appliances like rice cookers, slow cookers, and air fryers are great for cooking for one. They're easy to use and they can save you time and energy.

Get creative with your recipes.

There are many recipes that can be easily adapted to cook for one. For example, you can halve a recipe or make a one-pot meal.

Don't be afraid to experiment.

Cooking for one can be a great opportunity to experiment with new recipes and flavors. So don't be afraid to try something new.

Here are some additional tips on how to cook for one:

- Choose recipes that are easy to cook and that don't require a lot of ingredients. This will save you time and effort.
- Use kitchen tools that are designed for cooking for one. There are many kitchen tools that are specifically designed for cooking for one, such as mini muffin tins and single-serve rice cookers.
- Store your food properly. If you're cooking for one, it's important to store your food properly so that it doesn't go bad. Be sure to label your food and store it in airtight containers.
- Don't be afraid to ask for help. If you're not sure how to cook a certain dish or if you need help planning your meals,

don't be afraid to ask for help from a friend, family member, or cooking website.

By following these instructions, you can cook delicious and healthy meals for one.

How to cook for a crowd

Cooking for a crowd can be a daunting task, but it doesn't have to be! With a little planning and preparation, you can easily cook delicious and satisfying meals for a large group of people.

In this section, we'll discuss some ways to cook for a crowd. We'll cover topics such as choosing recipes that are appropriate for a large group, cooking different dishes at the same time, and managing your time effectively. We'll also provide some tips on how to set the mood and make your event a success.

Start with a plan.

Before you start cooking, take some time to plan your meal. This will help you to avoid wasting food and to make sure that you have everything you need.

Choose recipes that are easy to scale up.

There are many recipes that can be easily scaled up to cook for a crowd. For example, you can double or triple a recipe or make a one-pot meal that can easily be doubled or tripled.

Use large appliances.

Large appliances like ovens, stovetops, and grills are great for cooking for a crowd. They're able to cook large quantities of food quickly and easily.

Get creative with your serving dishes.

There are many ways to serve food to a crowd. You can use large platters, bowls, and trays. You can also use disposable dishes to make clean up easier.

Don't forget the sides.

When you're cooking for a crowd, it's important to have plenty of sides. This will help to fill everyone up and it will also add variety to your meal.

Be prepared to adjust your plans.

Things don't always go according to plan when you're cooking for a crowd. So be prepared to adjust your plans if necessary.

For example, you may need to cook more food than you originally planned or you may need to adjust the cooking time.

Don't be afraid to ask for help.

If you're not sure how to cook a certain dish or if you need help planning your meals, don't be afraid to ask for help from a friend, family member, or cooking website.

Keep in mind when cooking for a crowd:

- **Make sure you have enough seating.** If you're cooking for a large group, make sure you have enough seating. This will help to avoid people having to stand around and wait for food.
- **Have plenty of drinks on hand.** People will get thirsty when they're eating, so make sure you have plenty of drinks on hand. This could include water, soda, juice, or beer.
- **Decorate your table.** A beautifully decorated table can make your meal even more special. So take some time

to decorate your table with flowers, unscented candles (scented candles can ruin a meal), or other decorations.
- **Have fun!** Cooking for a crowd can be a lot of fun. So relax, enjoy the process, and let your guests know how much you appreciate them.

By following these tips, you can cook delicious and festive meals for a crowd.

Points to remember:

- It's important to follow instructions carefully when using a recipe. Experimenting and improving can be done after you know the basics.
- Don't let buzzwords and marketing gimmicks get you at the grocery store. Pay attention to the placement on the shelves and the placement of the claims on the packaging.
- Cooking for one or for a crowd can feel daunting, but with a little knowledge and preparation, you will be crushing it at both in no time!

Roommate Rules

HOW TO
BE A GOOD ROOMMATE &
HAVE HEALTHY RELATIONSHIPS

Chapter 7: Roommate Rules

"I'm not the easiest person to live with. I'm kind of a slob."

Katie Holmes

How to be a good roommate and have healthy relationships

Living with roommates can be a great way to save money and have companionship. However, it can also be challenging if you don't have clear rules and expectations.

This chapter will discuss some important roommate rules that can help you have a positive and healthy living experience.

We'll cover topics such as:

- **Communication**: How to communicate effectively with your roommates.
- **Cleanliness**: How to share a living space in a way that is fair and respectful.
- **Privacy**: How to balance your need for privacy with your roommate's needs.
- **Money**: How to discuss and manage shared expenses.
- **Conflict resolution**: How to resolve disagreements in a healthy way.

By following these rules, you can create a positive and healthy living environment for yourself and your roommates.

5 ways to be a good roommate

Want to make sure you're a good roommate? Follow these 5 fail proof roommate rules:

Respect your roommate's personal space

This means keeping your stuff out of their way, not borrowing their things without asking, and knocking before you enter their room.

Here are some surefire ways to ensure you're respecting your roommate's personal space!

- Keeping your stuff out of their way means being mindful of where you put your belongings. Don't leave your clothes, shoes, or other personal items strewn about the common areas. This can be a tripping hazard and it can also be annoying for your roommate if they have to constantly move your stuff around.
- Not borrowing their things without asking is a basic rule of thumb for being a good roommate. If you need to borrow something from your roommate, always ask first. Don't just take it without permission. This is especially important for things like

electronics, kitchen appliances, or other shared items.
- Knocking before you enter their room is a common courtesy that shows respect for your roommate's privacy. Even if your roommate is your best friend, it's always a good idea to knock before you enter their room. This gives them a chance to say if they're not up for company or if they're busy.

Be clean.

This means cleaning up after yourself in common areas, taking out the trash, and doing your fair share of the chores.

How can you be a mindful (instead of messy) roommate?

Cleaning up after yourself in common areas means taking care of your messes and not leaving them for your roommate to clean up. This includes things like:

- Putting your dishes in the dishwasher or sink after you use them.

- Taking out the trash when it's full.
- Sweeping or vacuuming the floor if you spill something.
- Picking up your clothes and other belongings.

Taking out the trash is another important part of being a clean roommate. This means taking the trash out on a regular basis, not just when it's overflowing. You should also make sure to properly dispose of any hazardous waste, such as batteries or cleaning products.

Doing your fair share of the chores is another important part of being a clean roommate. This means dividing up the chores evenly and taking responsibility for your assigned tasks. If you're not sure what your chores are, ask your roommate or create a chore chart together.

Here are some other tips for being a clean roommate:

- Mop the floors regularly.
- Dust the furniture.
- Wipe down the counters.

- Clean the bathroom.
- Take out the trash/recycling.

By following these suggestions, you can help to keep your shared space clean and tidy. This will make your home more comfortable for you and your roommate, and it will also help to prevent the spread of germs.

More tips for being a tidy roommate:

- **Set a good example.** If you see your roommate making a mess, offer to help them clean it up. This will show them that you're serious about keeping the place clean.
- **Be proactive.** Don't wait for the mess to build up before you clean it up. Take a few minutes each day to tidy up the common areas.
- **Be flexible.** If your roommate's schedule changes, be willing to adjust your chores accordingly.
- **Be positive.** Cleaning doesn't have to be a chore. Make it fun by listening to music or talking to your roommate while you're cleaning.

Follow these rules, and you'll be a clean roommate that creates a positive living environment for everyone.

Be quiet

This means keeping the noise down at night and during quiet hours, and being mindful of how loud you are when you're watching TV or listening to music.

Being considerate of your roommate's noise levels is important for creating a peaceful and harmonious living environment. This means being mindful of how loud you are, especially at night and during quiet hours.

Here are some ways to be considerate of your roommate's noise levels:

- Keep the noise down at night. This means turning down the volume on your TV or music, and avoiding loud activities, such as vacuuming or running the washing machine, late at night.
- Be mindful of how loud you are when you're talking on the phone. If you're

talking on the phone in a common area, try to keep your voice down so that you don't disturb your roommate.
- If you're having a party, let your roommate know in advance. This will give them a chance to prepare for the noise and decide if they want to stay home or go out.
- If you have noisy pets, be sure to take them outside during quiet hours. This will help to keep the noise down and prevent your roommate from being woken up by your pets.

Here are some additional tips for being considerate of your roommate's noise levels:

- Use headphones when you're listening to music or watching TV. This will prevent the sound from traveling through the walls and disturbing your roommate.
- Close the door to your room when you're making noise. This will help to keep the noise from traveling into the common areas.

- Be respectful of your roommate's sleep schedule. If you know that your roommate has to get up early for work, try to be quiet in the morning.

By following these rules, you can be considerate of your roommate's noise levels and create a peaceful living environment for everyone.

A few more things to keep in mind when it comes to noise levels:

- Everyone's noise tolerance is different. What might be considered "quiet" to you could be too loud for your roommate. It's important to be mindful of this and to adjust your behavior accordingly.
- There are different quiet hours in different places. In some places, quiet hours are from 10pm to 7am. In other places, they might be from 11pm to 8am. It's important to be aware of the quiet hours in your area and to respect them.
- If you're not sure what your roommate's noise tolerance is, ask

them. This is the best way to ensure that you're both comfortable with the noise levels in your shared space.

Communicate

Communication is key to having a successful roommate relationship. If you have a problem with your roommate, it's important to talk to them about it directly. Don't let things fester and turn into a big conflict.

Here are some ways to communicate effectively with your roommate:

- **Be direct.** Don't beat around the bush. Just tell your roommate what the problem is.
- **Be specific.** Don't just say "you're messy." Tell your roommate specifically what they're doing that's bothering you.
- **Be respectful.** Even if you're angry, try to be respectful of your roommate. Remember, you're still living together.
- **Be willing to compromise.** It's unlikely that you're going to get everything

you want. Be willing to compromise with your roommate so that you can both find a solution that works.
- **Be open to listening to your roommate's perspective.** They may have a different perspective on the problem than you do. Be open to hearing their side of things.

Here are some additional tips for communicating effectively with your roommate:

- Choose the right time and place to talk. Don't try to have a serious conversation when you're both stressed or tired.
- Be prepared to listen. Don't just talk *at* your roommate, talk *to* your roommate. Take the time to listen to what they have to say.
- Be willing to apologize. If you're wrong, be willing to apologize to your roommate.
- Be willing to forgive. If your roommate apologizes, be willing to forgive them.
- Don't wait until the problem is a big deal to talk about it. The sooner you

address the problem, the easier it will be to resolve.
- Don't be accusatory. Instead of saying "you always do this," try saying "I'm feeling frustrated when you do this."
- Focus on the problem, not the person. Don't attack your roommate personally. Stick to the issue at hand.
- Use "I" statements. This will help your roommate understand how their behavior is affecting you.
- Be open to feedback. Your roommate may have some feedback for you as well. Be open to hearing it and making changes if necessary.

Embrace open communication, and you will help to create a positive living environment for both of you.

Be willing to compromise

No two roommates are exactly alike, so there will be times when you have to compromise. Be willing to meet your roommate halfway so that you can both live comfortably.

Compromise is essential for having a successful roommate relationship. No two roommates are exactly alike, so there will be times when you have different expectations or preferences. When this happens, it's important to be willing to compromise so that you can both live comfortably.

How to compromise with your roommate:

- **Remember that you're both trying to make the best of a situation.** You're not trying to get one over on each other. You're both trying to find a way to live together that works for both of you.
- **Be willing to meet your roommate halfway.** This doesn't mean that you have to give up everything you want. It just means that you're willing to make some concessions in order to reach a mutually agreeable solution.
- **Be open to new ideas.** Your roommate may have some ideas for compromise that you hadn't thought of. Be open to hearing them and considering them.
- **Be willing to change your mind.** If you're not happy with the compromise

that you've reached, be willing to talk about it again and try to come up with a new solution.
- **Focus on the common ground.** What are the things that you and your roommate agree on? Start by focusing on those things and see if you can build a compromise around them.
- **Be creative.** Don't be afraid to think outside the box and come up with new and innovative solutions.
- **Be patient.** It may take some time to find a compromise that works for both of you. Be patient and keep working at it.

Here are some additional things to keep in mind when compromising with your roommate:

- **Don't be afraid to ask for help.** If you're stuck, don't be afraid to ask a friend, family member, or therapist for help.
- **Remember that compromise is a two-way street.** Both of you need to be

willing to compromise in order for it to work.
- **Don't give up.** If you're not able to reach a compromise right away, don't give up. Keep trying and eventually you'll find a solution that works for both of you.

The best way to avoid living in a toxic environment with your roommate is to be respectful, communicate openly, and be willing to compromise.

5 things you should avoid to be a good roommate

On the flip side, there are some things you should not be doing if you're trying to be a good roommate. Check out this list and see if you're guilty of any of these roommate faux pas!

Don't be a slob.

This means keeping your room clean, taking out the trash, and doing your fair share of the chores.

- **Don't leave your clothes, dishes, or other belongings strewn about the common areas.** This is a surefire way to annoy your roommate and make your living space look messy.
- **Don't let the trash pile up.** Take it out regularly, or make sure your roommate knows when it's their turn to take it out.
- **Don't avoid doing your fair share of the chores.** This is a great way to start a fight with your roommate.

By putting these on your "don'ts" list, you can avoid being a slob and create a more harmonious living environment for yourself and your roommate.

Here are some additional things to keep in mind:

- It's okay to have some mess in your room, but don't let it get out of control.

- If you're going to be gone for a few days, make sure to clean up before you leave.
- If you have a pet, make sure to take care of it and clean up after it.
- Don't be afraid to ask your roommate for help if you're feeling overwhelmed.

Showing your roommate that you're considerate of their needs and that you're willing to work together to keep the living space clean and tidy will go a long way in maintaining a good relationship!

Don't be noisy.

This means keeping the noise down at night and during quiet hours, and being mindful of how loud you are when you're watching TV or listening to music.

- Don't play music or watch TV too loudly, especially late at night. This can be very disruptive to your roommate's sleep, even if they're in a different room.
- Don't talk on the phone loudly in common areas. This is especially

important if your roommate is trying to study or work.
- Don't have loud parties or gatherings without letting your roommate know in advance. This is a surefire way to annoy them and make them feel uncomfortable in their own home.
- Don't use noisy appliances, such as the vacuum cleaner, the blender, or the washing machine, late at night. If you need to use these appliances, try to do it during the day when your roommate is less likely to be disturbed.

Avoid being noisy and create a more peaceful living environment for yourself and your roommate.

Here are some additional things to keep in mind:

- If you're not sure if your noise level is too high, ask your roommate. They'll be able to tell you if they're being disturbed by your noise.
- Be mindful of the noise levels in your neighborhood. If you live in a quiet

neighborhood, you'll want to be especially careful not to make too much noise.
- If you have a noisy pet, try to keep them quiet during the night and during quiet hours. You can do this by playing them calming music or giving them a chew toy to distract them.

By following these tips, you can show your roommate that you're considerate of their needs and that you're willing to work together to keep the living space peaceful.

Don't be disrespectful

This means not borrowing your roommate's things without asking, not entering their room without knocking, and not being rude or inconsiderate.

- **Don't borrow your roommate's things without asking.** This is a major no-no, and it's a surefire way to annoy your roommate.
- **Don't enter their room without knocking.** This is their personal space, and you should respect their privacy.

- **Don't be rude or inconsiderate.** This means not being loud or obnoxious, and not taking advantage of their kindness.
- **Don't make fun of their belongings or their interests.** This is a great way to start a fight.

By adding these to your "don'ts" list, you can avoid being disrespectful and create a more harmonious living environment for yourself and your roommate.

Here is some additional advice to keep in mind:

- If you need to borrow something from your roommate, ask them first. They'll be more likely to let you borrow it if you ask nicely.
- If you're going to be in your roommate's room, knock first and wait for them to say it's okay to come in. This is especially important if they're in the middle of something.
- Be mindful of your roommate's feelings. If you do something that you

think might be disrespectful, ask them if it was okay.
- Be willing to apologize if you make a mistake. Everyone makes mistakes, but it's important to be able to apologize and move on.

By showing your roommate that you respect them and that you're willing to work together to create a positive living environment, you will establish a happy and safe space for both of you.

Don't be passive-aggressive.

If you have a problem with your roommate, talk to them about it directly. Don't let things fester and turn into a big conflict.

- **Don't make snide comments or sarcastic remarks.** This is a passive-aggressive way of expressing your anger or frustration, and it's not going to solve anything.
- **Don't ignore your roommate or give them the silent treatment.** This is a surefire way to make them feel angry and resentful.

- **Don't do things to intentionally annoy your roommate,** such as leaving your dishes in the sink or taking up all the common space. This is passive-aggressive behavior, and it's not going to make your living situation any better.
- **Don't make promises you can't keep.** If you say you're going to do something, make sure you actually do it. Otherwise, your roommate is going to start to think that you're just blowing them off.

By following these rules, you can avoid being passive-aggressive and create a more communicative and respectful living environment for yourself and your roommate.

Here are a few more tidbits to keep in mind:

- If you have a problem with your roommate, talk to them about it directly. This is the best way to resolve the issue and avoid letting it fester.
- Be specific about what's bothering you. Don't just say "you're always

doing this." Instead, say something like "I feel frustrated when you leave your dishes in the sink."
- Be willing to listen to your roommate's perspective. They may have a different perspective on the issue than you do.
- Be willing to compromise. It's unlikely that you're going to get everything you want. Be willing to meet your roommate halfway so that you can both find a solution that works.

These tips will help you communicate effectively with your roommate and resolve any problems that may arise.

Don't be a mooch.

This means not expecting your roommate to pay for everything, and not taking advantage of their kindness.

- **Don't expect your roommate to pay for everything.** If you can't afford to pay for something, don't ask your roommate to pay for it for you.

- **Don't take advantage of your roommate's kindness.** If your roommate is always letting you borrow money or letting you use their things, be sure to pay them back or replace their things.
- **Don't be a freeloader.** If you're not contributing to the household expenses, don't expect your roommate to support you.
- **Don't be a burden.** If you're always asking your roommate for favors, they're going to start to feel like you're a burden.

If you follow these tips, you will be able to live with your roommate in a way that is mutually beneficial and respectful.

A few more things to keep in mind:

- **Be willing to pitch in.** If you're living with someone, it's important to be willing to pitch in and help out. This means paying your share of the rent and utilities, and also helping out with chores.

- **Be considerate of your roommate's financial situation.** If your roommate is struggling financially, don't ask them to pay for things that you can afford yourself.
- **Be grateful for your roommate's kindness.** If your roommate is always helping you out, be sure to thank them and let them know how much you appreciate their help.

By following these tips, you can show your roommate that you're not a mooch and that you're willing to contribute to the household.

Conclusion

Being a good roommate takes effort, but it's worth it. If you can be respectful, clean, considerate, and communicative, you'll be well on your way to having a great roommate experience.

I hope this has been helpful and gives you some wisdom and insights moving forward as you embark on your new cohabitation journey.

How to have healthy relationships

While having a good relationship with your roommate is very important, it's imperative to have healthy relationships with anyone in your life, whether that is a spouse or significant other, a boss, a family member, or a friend.

Here are some ways to avoid toxicity and surround yourself with positive and supportive people:

Set boundaries

Boundaries are important in any relationship, whether that be professional, platonic, or romantic. Boundaries help us to define what is acceptable behavior and what is not. They also help us to protect our own needs and feelings.

Here are some ways to set boundaries in your relationships:

- **Be clear about your needs and expectations.** What are you comfortable with? What are you not comfortable with?
- **Communicate your boundaries to your partner.** It's important to be open and honest about your needs and expectations.
- **Be willing to compromise.** Boundaries are not always black and white. Sometimes, you may need to compromise with your partner.
- **Be respectful of your partner's boundaries.** Just as you expect your partner to respect your boundaries, you should also respect their boundaries.

Be supportive:

Being supportive is an important part of any healthy relationship. It means being there for your partner when they need you, and it means being willing to listen to them and offer them your help.

Here are some ways you can be more supportive in your relationships:

- **Be a good listener.** When your partner is talking to you, really listen to what they are saying. Don't just wait for your turn to talk.
- **Offer your help.** If your partner is going through a tough time, offer to help them in any way you can.
- **Be positive and encouraging.** Let your partner know that you believe in them and that you are there for them.

Be honest:

Honesty is essential in any healthy relationship. It means being truthful with your partner, even when it's difficult.

Here are some suggestions for being honest in your relationships:

- **Be direct.** Don't beat around the bush. If you have something to say, say it directly.
- **Be respectful.** Even if you are being honest, you can still be respectful of your partner's feelings.
- **Be willing to apologize.** If you've said something that you shouldn't have, be willing to apologize to your partner.

I hope these fundamentals help you have healthy relationships. Remember, communication, respect, and honesty are key to success.

Additional resources on how to establish healthy relationships (and how to eliminate unhealthy ones):

- [8 Qualities of a True Friend](askmamaj.com/qualities-true-friend) –Ask Mama J: askmamaj.com/qualities-true-friend
- [Cutting Someone Out of Your Life for Good](askmamaj.com/cutting-someone-out-of-your-life-for-good-saying-goodbye-with-grace) –Ask Mama J: askmamaj.com/cutting-someone-out-of-your-life-for-good-saying-goodbye-with-grace

Points to remember:

- Respecting the space, privacy, noise levels, and boundaries of your roommate will contribute to long-term success.
- Being honest, supportive, and listening to your partner will help you have healthier relationships.

SELF CARE

HOW TO HAVE A POSITIVE MINDSET & PRIORITIZE TAKING CARE OF YOURSELF

Chapter 8: Self Care

"It's easy to forget yourself when there's always something to do. But you can't help anyone if you don't take care of you!"

Mama J

How to have a positive mindset & prioritize taking care of yourself

There's a silly little song I like to sing when teaching self care to others. The lines in the verses can pretty much be swapped out to anything you want them to be, as long as you rhyme the 3rd line with "self care."

It goes a little something like this:

Self Care Song

©2021 Jessica Bowman. All rights reserved.

Verse 1:

Make a budget

Take a walk

Fix your hair

Self care

Take a shower

Meditate

Say a prayer

Self Care

Chorus:

It's easy to forget yourself

when there's always something to do

But you can't help anyone

if you don't take care of you

Self Care!

Verse 2:

Get a footbath

Exfoliate

Go to the fair

Self Care

Do a kindness

Watch a movie

Dance in the square

Self Care

Chorus:

It's easy to forget yourself

when there's always something to do

But you can't help anyone

if you don't take care of you

You can do anything you want to

Self Care!

Self Care!

Self Care!

Self Care!

What is self care?

Self-care is the practice of taking care of your physical, mental, and emotional health. It is important to take care of yourself because it allows you to function at your best and to cope with stress and challenges.

There are many different ways to practice self-care. Some common self-care activities include:

- Getting enough sleep.
- Eating a healthy diet.
- Exercising regularly.
- Spending time in nature.
- Reading.
- Listening to music.
- Taking a bath or shower.
- Meditating or practicing yoga.
- Spending time with loved ones.

Taking care of your physical health

Your physical health is important because it affects your overall well-being. When you take care of your physical health, you are more likely to have energy, feel good, and be able to cope with stress.

Some ways to take care of your physical health include:

- **Getting enough sleep.** Adults need around 7-8 hours of sleep per night.
- **Eating a healthy diet.** This means eating plenty of fruits, vegetables, and whole grains.
- **Exercising regularly.** Aim for at least 30 minutes of moderate-intensity exercise most days of the week.
- **Maintaining a healthy weight.** Being overweight or obese can increase your risk of developing chronic health conditions.

- Getting regular medical checkups. This is important for catching any health problems early.

Taking care of your mental health

Your mental health is just as important as your physical health. When you take care of your mental health, you are more likely to feel good, be able to cope with stress, and have a positive outlook on life.

Some ways to take care of your mental health include:

- **Practicing relaxation techniques.** This could include meditation, yoga, or deep breathing exercises.
- **Spending time with loved ones.** Social support is important for your mental health.
- **Engaging in activities you enjoy.** This could be anything from reading to playing sports to spending time in nature.
- **Resetting the tape in your brain.** You know, the one that tells you you're

ugly, stupid, not good enough, etc. By telling that voice to stop lying and re-recording the tape to say more positive things, you will take care of yourself from the inside out.
- **Seeking professional help if needed.** If you are struggling with your mental health, don't be afraid to seek professional help. A therapist can help you develop coping mechanisms and strategies for managing your mental health.

Remember #988: The new three-digit number for mental health crisis. Dial #988 or text HOME to 741741 to connect with a trained counselor 24/7. You're not alone.

Taking care of your emotional health

Your emotional health is also important. When you take care of your emotional health, you are more likely to feel happy, balanced, and able to cope with difficult emotions.

Some ways to take care of your emotional health include:

- **Acknowledge your emotions.** It's okay to feel a range of emotions, both positive and negative.
- **Express your emotions in a healthy way.** This could mean talking to a friend, singing, journaling, or exercising. Find a way to let it all out without taking it out on loved ones.
- **Practice self-compassion.** Be kind to yourself and forgive yourself for mistakes.
- **Set boundaries.** Don't be afraid to say no to things that you don't want to do.
- **Take time for yourself.** This could mean reading, taking a bath, or doing something else that you enjoy.

I hope this helps you understand the importance of self-care and how to practice it in your own life. Remember, self-care is an ongoing process, and it's important to find what works best for you.

Prioritizing self care

Self-care is important for everyone, but it can be especially difficult to prioritize when you're busy and stressed. However, making time for self-care is essential for your physical and mental health.

In this section, we'll discuss the importance of self-care and how to prioritize it in your life. We'll cover topics such as making time for things that really matter to you, saying no to things that aren't serving you, and prioritizing your own needs.

Making time for the things that make you happy

One of the best ways to prioritize self-care is to make time for the things that make you happy. This could mean reading, spending time in nature, listening to music, or doing something else that you enjoy.

When you do things that make you happy, you release endorphins, which have mood-boosting effects. You also get to relax and de-stress, which is essential for your overall well-being.

Saying no to things that aren't important

Another way to prioritize self-care is to say no to things that aren't important. This could mean saying no to extra work, social engagements, or other commitments that you don't have time for or that don't make you happy.

It can be difficult to say no, but it's important to remember that you don't have to do everything that's asked of you. If you're feeling overwhelmed, it's okay to say no.

Here are some tips for saying no:

- **Be honest about your reasons.** Don't make up excuses.

- **Be direct and assertive.** Don't beat around the bush.
- **Be respectful.** Even if you're saying no, be polite and respectful of the other person's feelings.
- **Be prepared for push back.** Some people may try to pressure you into saying yes. Be prepared to stand your ground.

Prioritize your own needs

Finally, it's important to prioritize your own needs. This means putting yourself first sometimes and doing things that are good for you, even if it means saying no to other people's requests.

It's easy to get caught up in taking care of others, but it's important to remember that you need to take care of yourself first. If you're not taking care of yourself, you won't be able to take care of others effectively.

Here are some helpful methods to prioritize your own needs:

- **Schedule time for yourself.** This could mean setting aside time each day for relaxation or exercise.
- **Learn to say no.** It's okay to say no to requests that aren't important to you.
- **Delegate tasks.** If you have too much on your plate, don't be afraid to delegate tasks to others.
- **Take breaks.** If you're feeling overwhelmed, take a break. Go for a walk, listen to music, or do something else that you enjoy.

I hope these suggestions help you prioritize self-care in your own life. Remember, you're important, too!

Living life with a positive mindset

What's up with those "glass half full" people, and why are they always so darn chipper?

The truth is, while those people might be annoying to you, they are not worried about that at all. Bad things happen to everyone, but the happiest people are the ones who look for the good in bad things, pick themselves up, dust themselves off, and keep moving forward.

Focus on the good

One of the best ways to have a positive mindset is to focus on the good. This means paying attention to the positive things in your life and in the world around you.

When you focus on the good, you're more likely to feel happy and optimistic. You're also more likely to be grateful for what you have and to see the silver lining in difficult situations.

Practice an attitude of gratitude

Gratitude is a powerful emotion that can have a positive impact on your mindset. When you're grateful, you focus on the good things in your life and you appreciate what you have.

Gratitude can also help you cope with difficult times. When you're grateful for the good things in your life, it's easier to see the silver lining in difficult situations.

Here are some ways to start practicing gratitude:

- **Keep a gratitude journal.** Every day, write down three things you're grateful for.
- **Spend time with people who are grateful.** When you're around people who are grateful, it's more likely that you'll feel grateful yourself.
- **Do things that make you feel grateful.** When you do things that make you

feel grateful, you're more likely to focus on the good in your life.

See the silver lining

In difficult situations, there is often a silver lining. When you can see the silver lining, it's easier to stay positive and hopeful. I call this the "lessons and blessings" (spoken with a Southern accent, so it rhymes).

Even in the most difficult times, being able to find that silver lining, the lessons and blessings, can help you get through it and see the value in the experience, no matter how awful it may have been at the time.

Here are some tips for seeing the silver lining:

- **Ask yourself, "What could I learn from this?"** Difficult situations can often teach us valuable lessons. When you can see the silver lining, you're more likely to be able to learn from the experience and grow as a person.

- **Focus on the positive aspects of the situation.** Even in difficult situations, there are often some positive aspects. When you can focus on the positive, it's easier to stay positive and hopeful.
- **Remember that you're not alone.** Everyone experiences difficult times. When you remember that you're not alone, it's easier to cope with the situation.

I hope this will help you have a positive mindset in your own life. Remember, it's okay to have negative thoughts sometimes, but it's important to focus on the positive and to be grateful for what you have.

Points to remember:

- If you don't take care of and love yourself, you will not be able to effectively take care of and love others without exhaustion and resentment.
- #988 is the new three-digit number for mental health crises. Dial #988 or

text HOME to 741741 to connect with a trained counselor 24/7. You're not alone.
- Look for the lessons and blessings in every setback, failure, and difficult experience.

SUMMARY

WHERE TO GO FROM HERE

Chapter 9: Summary

"You are awesome. That is all."

Mama J

What you've learned in this book:

Hooray, we're almost finished! Hopefully all of the information in this book has helped you to feel a little less alone and equipped you with knowledge and confidence moving into the adult world.

To recap, here's what we've learned so far:

- **What does it mean to be an adult?** In this chapter, we discussed the different aspects of adulthood, such as taking responsibility for your actions, and the challenges that may

arise. We also talked about the importance of being self-aware and setting realistic expectations for yourself.
- **How to get organized:** In this chapter, we discussed the importance of being organized and how to create a system that works for you. We also talked about the different tools and resources that can help you stay organized.
- **How to land your dream job:** In this chapter, we discussed the steps involved in finding and landing your dream job. We talked about the importance of networking, preparing for interviews, and following up after interviews. We also talked about the importance of being positive and believing in yourself.
- **How to manage money:** In this chapter, we discussed the basics of financial management, such as creating a budget, saving for the future, and paying off debt. We also talked about the importance of being mindful of your spending and making informed financial decisions.

- **Cleaning 101:** In this chapter, we discussed the basics of cleaning, such as how to create a cleaning routine, how to tackle large projects, and how to keep your home clean on a daily basis. We also talked about the importance of decluttering and getting rid of unnecessary items.
- **Cooking 101:** In this chapter, we discussed the basics of cooking, such as how to cook a basic meal, how to use kitchen tools, and how to grocery shop. We also broke down all the scary kitchen terms and shared ways to avoid grocery store marketing traps!
- **How to be a good roommate:** In this chapter, we discussed the importance of communication, respect, and compromise when living with roommates. We also talked about the importance of setting boundaries, establishing ground rules, and carrying that forward into all of your relationships.
- **Taking care of yourself and having a positive attitude:** In this chapter, we discussed the importance of taking care of your physical and mental health. We talked about the

importance of eating healthy, exercising, and protecting your mental health. We also talked about the importance of having a positive attitude and believing in yourself.

How to apply what you've learned:

Take what you've learned from this book and apply it to many different areas of your life. For example, the tips on how to get organized can help you in your personal and professional life. The tips on how to manage money can help you save for the future and achieve your financial goals. And the tips on how to cook can help you save money and eat healthier.

Where to go from here:

The information in this book is just a starting point. There are many other resources available to help you learn more about adulting. You can find books, articles, websites, and even online courses that can teach you more about the topics covered in this book.

About Ask Mama J

Ask Mama J began when our foster parent journey ended in 2021. While I wanted to adopt both boys we had fostered, both boys were ultimately reunited with their birth families. I was happy for them, but there was definitely a giant hole in my heart.

I began writing letters to them both as they grew up, incorporating different practical lessons and love and encouragement.

Later in 2021, my uncle passed away from a sudden bout of cancer. My cousin, a young adult, came to live with me after losing his dad. It was clear that he had not learned the proper tools needed to leave the nest and survive in the real world.

I began sharing the lessons I had written down for our foster boys, and writing additional lessons as questions came up, such as "why do we fold clothes?"

After many conversations, I learned that my cousin was not alone, that there were many teenagers and young adults who had not received the knowledge or support needed to leave the nest and make it in the real world. As I reflected, I remembered all of the times where I felt so lost when I was just starting out, too. And so Ask Mama J was born.

AskMamaJ.com is a hub for young adults who are just getting started in the real world. Mama J has seen it all, and she is here to offer helpful tips on everything from finding a job to dealing with relationships to navigating the adult world.

Whether you're feeling lost and confused or just need some guidance, Ask Mama J is an online community and safe space for you. I am here to encourage, empower, and equip you with the tools you need to succeed.

I'm here to help you understand all the adult lingo and jargon, and WHY certain things are important. I'm here to help break down everything that sounds super scary to you right NOW, so that it will become second-nature to you.

I'm here to help you worry LESS about how to perform basic adult tasks, so you can spend MORE time figuring out how to live a happy and healthy life, doing the things you want to do, surrounded by people who love and encourage you.

- Even if life has been unkind to you so far.
- Even if you have been bullied, abused, or neglected.
- Even if failure has never been an option for you.
- Even if you think your life is already planned out.
- And especially even if you barely survived childhood and adolescence

and worry that you might not make it to 25.

I'm here to tell you that it's not just going to be OK, but it's going to be AMAZING! Life doesn't have to be what other people tell you it is. It can be the most fun and beautiful journey.

You CAN live your dreams. You CAN land on your feet. But you can also fall flat on your face, and that's actually good, too. The key is learning to pick yourself up and try again, or try something else.

I'm here to help you write YOUR OWN story.

Every week, I'll address the struggles and issues that you're facing right now. I'll teach you the basics but also encourage and empower you to succeed and live your best life. I'll be that kooky-but-kind bonus mom that you can look to in times of trouble and in times of need.

There are no stupid questions. Forgive yourself right now for not knowing what you don't know, okay? I'm here to cheer you on, help build your confidence, give you tough love when needed, and give you grace for making mistakes. Think of me as a really colorful set of training wheels...that you want to hug.

Sign up to join the Ask Mama J community here: AskMamaJ.com/Community

The most important thing is to start learning and taking action. The more you learn and the more you practice, the better you will become at adulting. So don't be afraid to get started!

CONCLUSION

**CONGRATS! YOU'RE READY
GO OUT THERE & START ADULTING!**

Chapter 10: Conclusion

"Then everything is wrapped up in a neat little package."

Homer Simpson

Congratulations on finishing this book!

I hope you found it helpful. This book has covered a lot of ground, from the basics of adulthood to more specific topics like managing money and cooking. I hope you have learned some new things and that you feel more confident about taking on the challenges of adulthood.

Other helpful resources:

In addition to this book, there are many other resources available to help you learn more about entering the adult world. Here are a few suggestions:

- AskMamaJ.com - Community and safe space for young adults
- CommonSense.org-Life skills and adulting resources
- ActforYouth.net-Adult preparation toolkit

Now go out there and start adulting!

The most important thing is to start learning and taking action. The more you learn and the more you practice, the better you will become at adulting. So don't be afraid to get started!

I wish you all the best in your adulting journey!

Love, Mama J

Acknowledgements

Thank you to everyone who helped me with this book and to those who have believed in me and inspired me to become a writer.

To God, for giving me this gift. I didn't become a writer, I have always been a writer. I know this is Your plan and for Your glory. (I'm sorry I swear so much!)

To my mom, for always making sure I had plenty of books to read and notebooks and journals to write in. I believe the writer gene was passed down from her DNA.

To my teachers, and to the late great Dave Weinthal for believing in me and encouraging me. And for printing some of the craziest stories that should never have made it to print!

To my counselor, Melissa, for always giving it to me straight and helping me see the places where I've been hard on myself and soft on others, allowing me to set boundaries and get out of my own way.

To my support network who said I should get over myself and my fears and just go for it! Thank you so much to my husband Joey, and to Rachel, Stacey, Vann, and Maegan, for helping to make this the most valuable book it can be.

To my mentor Ruth, for teaching me many of these lessons I have now shared with you, and for believing I could do so much more than even I thought I could do. One of the most valuable lessons she ever taught me was "focus on what you have to give, not how you will be perceived." That is how this book exists.

To all my haters, whose negative energy motivates me more than any other thing to counteract with my positive energy. Nothing fuels my fire more than this, so thank you!

And last but definitely not least to you, the reader, for inspiring this book into existence. Your questions and struggles helped this book write itself, and I am so grateful for you and hope that this helps make life seem a little less scary on your adulting journey.

About the Author

A former foster parent, Jessica Bowman began writing down life skills and other important lessons to share with her kids as they grew up.

When a young family member came to live with her in 2021 after a death in the family, Jessica realized that there were many young adults who were not properly prepared for adulthood, thus Mama J was born. She aims to help provide the training wheels needed to bridge the gap between childhood and adulthood for teens and young adults, so they feel less overwhelmed and more prepared for success.

Jessica lives with her husband, Joel and several furry and feathered creatures in Dade County, GA.

Printed in Great Britain
by Amazon